# Developing Inclusive Schooling

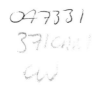

## The Bedford Way Papers Series

# Developing Inclusive Schooling: Perspectives, policies and practices

*Edited by*
*Carol Campbell*

**Bedford Way Papers**

INSTITUTE OF
EDUCATION
UNIVERSITY OF LONDON

First published in 2002 by the Institute of Education, University of London,
20 Bedford Way, London WC1H 0AL
www.ioe.ac.uk

*Pursuing Excellence in Education*

© Institute of Education, University of London 2002

**British Library Cataloguing in Publication Data:**
A catalogue record for this publication is available from the British Library

ISBN 0 85473 648 4

Design and typography by Joan Rose
Cover design by Andrew Chapman
Page make-up by Cambridge Photosetting Services, Cambridge

Production services by
Book Production Consultants plc, Cambridge

Printed by Watkiss Studios, Biggleswade, Beds

# Contents

# Authors

The authors are all based at the Institute of Education, University of London. Carol Campbell is Lecturer in Education Management; David Gillborn is Professor of Education; Ingrid Lunt is Reader in Educational Psychology and Assistant Dean of Research; Pamela Sammons is Professor of Education and Co-ordinating Director of the International School Effectiveness and School Improvement Centre; Carol Vincent is Senior Lecturer in Education Policy; Simon Warren is Research Officer in the Education Policy Research Unit; Geoff Whitty is Professor of Education and Director of the Institute of Education.

# Acknowledgements

I would like to thank the Scottish Executive Education Department for funding the research project, 'A Review of Developments in Inclusive Schooling'. I would like to thank also the following colleagues for their advice and assistance: Dr Kelly Coate, Cate Knowles, Dr Pat Petrie, Gill Poland, Professor Sally Power and Pamela Robertson.

# Introduction

*Carol Campbell*

The term 'inclusive schooling' has risen in prominence both internationally and within the UK during recent years. However, what constitutes inclusive schooling and how such an approach should be developed at the national, local and school levels is contested and complex.

As a term, inclusive schooling has been closely associated with the movement to include pupils designated as having special educational needs into 'mainstream' schools. However, recently the term has been used more widely to refer to 'inclusive schooling for all', broadening its scope to include new areas of concern. The focus is on tackling all forms of discrimination, disadvantage and exclusionary processes. This conceptualisation emphasises 'inclusive schooling' as being linked to social justice and social inclusion. It raises questions about equity of access to schooling, equity of treatment within schools and equity of outcomes from schooling. These changing definitions are further explored in Chapter 1 and are central to the issues raised and evidence presented throughout this edited collection.

The focus of this volume is mainly on inclusive schooling and the need to examine the inclusive, exclusive and discriminatory processes and outcome of schools. However, questions concerning inclusive schooling are closely linked to wider political, social and economic debates. As Armstrong *et al.* (2000: 1) note: 'Whilst educational policies and practices are the particular focus of examination, the fundamental interest is in the realisation of an inclusive society.' This aspiration is set against a context of unacceptable inequalities and exclusionary processes affecting both education and society more widely.

Tracing the shifts in social and economic inequalities, Pantazis explains:

The growing divide between the poor and the rich is probably the most significant social change to have occurred under 18 years of Conservative government. The New Labour government inherited a country more unequal than at any other time since the Second World War (Barclay, 1995; Hills, 1995; 1998...). There are now wider gaps in income inequality between different family types, different economic status groups, different housing tenures, and between different regions (Goodman et al., 1997; Hills 1998).... Compared with other European countries, the United Kingdom (UK) now has the highest proportion of children living in households where income is below half that of the average (Eurostat, 1997) – or what is generally considered as the best proxy for an official poverty line.

Despite the overall growth in incomes under the previous Conservative governments, rates of growth were not shared equally throughout the population. The Households Below Average Income (HBAI) statistics demonstrate that whereas the income of the richest 10% of the population grew from 60% to 68% between 1979 and 1994/95, the income of the poorest group grew by only 10% (before housing costs) or fell by 8% if calculated after housing costs (Hills, 1998). Some groups – including children – have become worse off in absolute terms.

(Pantazis, 2000: 1)

While Pantazis (2000) notes that there has been a reduction in income inequality since the mid-1990s, the Social Exclusion Unit (SEU, 2001) continues to indicate the unacceptable levels of poverty and exclusion in England and particularly as affecting children.

Concerns about current levels of inequality and exclusion have been linked to economic and social changes. The Social Exclusion Unit (2001) outlines economic changes and their consequences for labour markets, including changing skills requirements and the growth of the 'knowledge-economy' creating new demands for an educated workforce (the implications for gender and inclusive schooling are discussed in Chapter 4). The SEU (2001) points also to social changes, including polarised communities and changing family structures (the issues arising for parental involvement in education are noted in Chapter 5). The current UK New Labour government are promoting the importance of developing and combining both economic competitiveness and social cohesion; although tensions in practice and principle in securing both have been noted (see Pantazis, 2000). As is discussed in Chapter 1, the Social Exclusion Unit has been established to tackle exclusionary processes and inequitable outcomes. Evaluations conducted by the SEU suggest that some previous government working practices, for example fragmentation between areas of social and economic policy requiring 'joined up' solutions, may have contributed to the problem and that the work of the Unit is beginning to make some difference (SEU, 2001). Nevertheless, there have been concerns that New Labour have emphasised equality of opportunity without adequate attention to the issues of equality of outcome and that an assumption that increasing 'opportunities' will remove inequalities may be misplaced (see Pantazis, 2000). Chapter 1 considers the definitions of equality and their linkage to concerns about social justice.

There has been considerable debate about the extent to which inclusive and exclusive processes within schooling can be distanced and disentangled from wider structures and processes of social inclusion and exclusion in society. The impact of indicators of social disadvantage on educational outcomes is significant and must be considered alongside research on 'school effects'. Therefore, although schools are important in the development of social inclusion, they are not the only element in reforming appropriate social and economic policies. Nevertheless, research internationally points to the important roles and impacts of schools.

The linkages between promoting social inclusion are fundamental to current debates about 'inclusive schooling'. As indicated previously, this is a broader definition than a focus only on the 'inclusion' of children designated as having 'special education needs' in 'mainstream' provision (involving their educational and social inclusion, rather than simply their physical integration). As discussed throughout this collection, there is growing support for the conceptualisation and practice of inclusion for *all*. As Armstrong *et al.* comment:

> In taking this approach it is important to recognise that inclusive education is not an end in itself. Nor ultimately is the fundamental issue

that of disabled people. In educational terms it is about the value
and well-being of all pupils. Thus, the key concern is about how, where
and with what consequences do we educate all children and young
people. This inevitably involves both a desire for, and engagement
with, the issue of change (Daniels and Garner 1999, Ballard 1999,
Thrupp 1999).

(Armstrong *et al.*, 2000: 1)

This conception of inclusive schooling as concerning multiple forms of
disadvantage and discrimination is relatively recent. Discussing the
development of the Warnock Report, which has been central to ongoing
educational developments for children designated as having 'special
education needs', Mary Warnock has since commented:

> Looking back on the days of the committee, when everyone felt that a
> new world was opening for disadvantaged children, the most strikingly
> absurd fact is that the committee was forbidden to count social depri-
> vation as in any way contributing to educational needs. ... The very idea
> of such a separation now seems preposterous.
>
> (Warnock, 1999, cited in Clough and Corbett, 2000: 4)

The need to consider inclusive schooling in terms of the range of exclusionary and discriminatory processes is a central theme of this edited
collection. Nevertheless, as will be discussed, there remain tensions between
a broad definition of inclusive schooling and the need also to consider the
needs of specific groups of children. And while current UK government
policy has considered the development of 'inclusion' in education, tensions
have been identified between the promotion of inclusion and the drive for
standards, and the promotion of social cohesion alongside market forces
in education (see Thomas and Loxley, 2001).

There remain different perspectives concerning 'inclusive schooling'.
As Clough and Corbett (2000: 14) have indicated: 'There is finally no
single, enduring version which – transcendentally, as it were – pervades the
history of inclusive education.' Rather, they suggest: '"Inclusion" is not a
single movement, it is made up of many strong currents of belief, many different local struggles and a myriad forms of practice' (2000: 6). Yet they

consider that there may be: 'Some recent convergence of thinking about inclusion, about what it is – or should be – and about how it will be best achieved ... a convergence of energies of different sorts in the project of inclusion' (2000: 29). The need to explore the range of perspectives associated with inclusion and for serious debate and dialogue to potentially develop new perspectives and futures for 'inclusive schooling' has been advocated (see for example, Booth and Ainscow, 1998; Corbett and Slee, 2000). This edited collection brings together a range of issues and perspectives concerning inclusive schooling to contribute to such a debate.

The current debate concerning 'inclusive schooling', and more widely social inclusion, has been stimulated by a range of political, social, economic and educational factors. Shifts in the focus and conceptualisation of researchers have been influential also in broadening the debate concerning inclusion and challenging constructions of disability and special needs. As Thomas and Loxley explain:

> Changes have been possible in thinking about inclusion in education not only because of changes in the social climate, but also (and perhaps more significantly), because of changes in the way that 'difficulty' is conceptualised; there seems far less willingness now to locate the difficulties which children may experience at school unproblematically in the children themselves – whether the 'in-ness' be about children's learning or behaviour, or about their social background, family income, gender or race.
>
> In the next few years there is likely to be an extension of the changes which took place at the end of the twentieth century, with an increasing recognition of the interconnectedness of the issues which surround inclusion. Increasingly, these interconnected issues will be dealt with outside the professional and disciplinary boundaries once set.
>
> (Thomas and Loxley, 2001: 124)

An important feature of this edited collection is to bring together a range of disciplines and perspectives to examine the range of issues and evidence associated with developing truly inclusive schooling.

## Structure of the book

This edited collection provides an overview of significant developments
and summarises emerging research findings relevant to perspectives,
policies and practices associated with this broadened definition of inclusive schooling. Evidence from the UK, Europe, North America and
Australia is presented. However, the conceptualisation of social exclusion,
social inclusion and inclusive schooling varies between countries. The
many differences in the educational, political, cultural and economic systems among the countries from which we draw evidence make direct
comparisons of policies and practices problematic. Furthermore, the
chapters vary in the presentation of international evidence depending on
their field of enquiry and the extent to which relevant developments for
inclusive schooling can be drawn on from different countries. This
review, therefore, is based on a thematic framework providing an
overview and synthesis of issues and strategies pertinent to inclusive
schooling, including:

- special educational needs;
- 'race' and ethnicity;
- gender;
- parental involvement;
- inter-agency working;
- school effectiveness and school improvement research.

This edited collection arises from a research project reviewing developments in inclusive schooling funded by the Scottish Executive Education
Department; therefore our remit focuses particularly on policies and
practices relating to school-age children in primary and secondary schools.
However, inclusive educational practices apply to the full range of educational activities and learning opportunities, from pre-school to ongoing
lifelong learning. There is a need for further research on the linkages
between inclusive schooling for school-age children, early years pre-
school education and transitions post-school.

As previously indicated, there is no single agreed definition of inclusive schooling. It is a concept that is growing in prominence and is therefore continuing to develop. Chapter 1 provides an overview of the developing definitions of inclusive schooling, linked particularly to special educational needs, social justice, social exclusion, social inclusion, school effectiveness, school improvement, and arguments about the reform of schooling. This range of foci is important, since different disciplines have different perspectives on inclusion which can sometimes be in tension. Chapters 2, 3 and 4 provide an overview of developments relating to specific forms of exclusionary and inclusionary processes within schools relating to special educational needs (Chapter 2), 'race' and ethnicity (Chapter 3) and gender (Chapter 4). An evaluation of existing research and current strategies in these areas is provided.

In Chapter 2, Ingrid Lunt explains that inclusive schooling is complex in relation to special educational needs, raising questions about values, rights and equity. While the principle of inclusion is widely supported, there is debate as to whether full inclusion involving the placing of all pupils in 'mainstream' schools should be the aim. There are tensions between principled arguments based on human rights and equality, and pragmatic arguments for the most appropriate education to meet individual needs. It is explained that evidence suggests that there may be a minority of pupils designated as having complex and severe special needs for whom specialist provision could be necessary beyond that which could be funded and sustained in a mainstream setting. The maintenance of two systems of provision, however, raises questions of the right to choose where to be educated and the distribution of resources. Lunt evaluates outcomes associated with inclusive schooling for children designated as having special educational needs and discusses strategies and features associated with inclusive schooling.

In Chapter 3, David Gillborn reviews issues for inclusive schooling associated with a consideration of 'race' and ethnicity. An appreciation of ethnic diversity and an awareness of anti-racism are increasingly recognised as essential components of a 'good' education, regardless of the particular ethnic mix in a school. Therefore, multicultural and anti-racist approaches are important across the curriculum, where they should inform teaching and content in all subject areas. Attention needs to be paid also to language issues and developing appropriate approaches to community languages and bilingualism for pupils and their families. Gillborn evaluates the impact of classroom structures and teachers' expectations for the experiences of minority ethnic students. Clear and consistent policies on racism are required. Policies, practices and strategies associated with developing inclusive schooling in a multi-ethnic society are reviewed.

In Chapter 4, Simon Warren discusses inclusive schooling in relation to gender. The current emphasis on boys' relative underachievement is considered. Triggers for change in gender equity in schooling are reviewed. Warren suggests that consideration of gender and education cannot focus only on outcomes, but must consider also processes within schooling (for example, in classroom practices and interaction). There are problems with approaches which focus specifically on behaviour rather than consideration also of curriculum reform, including what is taught, how it is taught and the materials used. Warren raises concerns about some current approaches to gender and education. Goals and approaches associated with developing gender reform work in schools are discussed.

Although the focus is mainly on in-school strategies and processes, research suggests the need to develop partnerships and collaboration with parents, communities and other agencies, both involving them within schools and schooling, and extending the external linkages of schools.

Chapter 5 reviews developments and strategies relating to parental involvement. While developing a partnership between home and school, is widely advocated, the realisation of this partnership can be difficult and a range of different approaches has been suggested. Carol Vincent reviews current key policies and practices in this area and evaluates related evidence. Vincent offers recommendations for further developing parental involvement in terms of the capacity for individual voice and collective voice.

Chapter 6 evaluates different purposes, practices and outcomes associated with school-linked inter-agency collaboration. It is increasingly recognised that, if schooling is to become more inclusive, schools must

further develop new ways of working with other agencies. Such developments emphasise that a pupil's educational achievement cannot easily be
separated from their personal, social, emotional and physical development and well-being. Collaboration is required as existing services and
supports can be highly fragmented. Carol Campbell and Geoff Whitty
review evaluations and evidence relating to a range of practices involving
school-linked inter-agency collaboration, for example healthy schools in
England and full service schools in the USA. A range of purposes and
approaches associated with the further development of collaborations are
considered.

Chapters 2 to 6, therefore, provide an overview and analysis of
research, issues and strategies which are relevant to the development of
inclusive schooling. However, with the current emphasis on effectiveness
in the UK, there is debate as to whether inclusive schools can also be
effective schools. Chapter 7 focuses specifically on the nature and development of school effectiveness research and school improvement approaches,
and their linkages to the processes, outcomes and evaluations of 'inclusive
schooling'. Pam Sammons considers the role of school effectiveness
research in identifying the differential effectiveness of schools for different
groups of pupils, for example based on an analysis of gender, ethnicity
and/or socio-economic status. Sammons discusses the complexity of
understanding effectiveness and the need to evaluate pupil progress in
terms of social, affective and cognitive outcomes. Research about school
effectiveness and school improvement relevant to the development of
inclusive schooling, particularly for schools in disadvantaged areas, is
reviewed. From this, Sammons identifies a number of strategies associated with effective, improving and inclusive schooling.

The final chapter, Chapter 8, provides a synthesis of key strategies and
issues arising from the previous chapters. While inclusive schools may
share features of healthy schools, child-friendly schools, improving
schools and effective schools, in themselves these features are not necessarily sufficient to create an inclusive school where the focus must be on
inclusive policies, practices, processes and outcomes. There is a need to
consider both whole school strategies which all schools could adopt

(such as anti-sexism and anti-racism across the curriculum) and the need for targeted and localised strategies depending on pupil and school needs. Furthermore, while schools can and do make a difference, it is well established that social disadvantage impacts significantly on educational outcomes. Therefore, to promote social and educational inclusion, inclusive schooling is a significant development which must be considered alongside wider social and economic policies. The need for further research concerning the development and evaluation of inclusive schooling is advocated.

# 1 Conceptualisations and definitions of inclusive schooling

*Carol Campbell*

The concept of 'inclusive schooling' has grown in prominence, particularly during the past decade. However, this rise in prominence has not necessarily been associated with increased clarity as to the definition of inclusive schooling and associated policies and practices. Rather, what constitutes inclusive schooling and how such an approach should be developed in policy and practice at national, local and school levels is contested and complex. Therefore, this chapter provides a broad overview of concepts relevant to inclusive schooling and proposed definitions of inclusive schooling. Such conceptualisations and definitions are further developed throughout this book. The purpose of this chapter is not to offer one conclusive definition of inclusive schooling, but rather to illustrate the complexity of the concept and the range of different potential interpretations. As indicated in the introduction, the development of perspectives, policies and practices for inclusive schooling must be considered within the wider political, social and economic context and changing conceptions, processes and outcomes of discrimination and disadvantage. The focus of this chapter is the shifting definitions of 'inclusive schooling' and their linkage to wider changes in conceptions of education and disadvantage.

The specific term 'inclusive schooling' has been most closely associated with the movement towards the 'inclusion' of pupils designated as having special educational needs into 'mainstream' schooling. Within this perspective, a focus on specific individual needs is vital. This focus on individual needs has been developed in an expanded definition of inclusive schooling to incorporate meeting the individual needs of all pupils. However, there needs to be attention also to the diverse needs of individuals and groups of pupils, for example related to processes and outcomes of disadvantage and discrimination. Hence, any definition of inclusive schooling should take account of issues of social justice and injustice. 'Inclusion' is not simply about equality of access to schooling, but also equality of circumstance, participation and outcomes. The associations between inclusionary and exclusionary processes and outcomes at school and societal levels must be explored. Therefore, there is a need to investigate the interconnections between social disadvantage and educational processes and outcomes. The extent to which school improvements and school effects can contribute to extending inclusionary processes and reducing exclusionary ones requires careful analysis. There are debates as to whether 'inclusive schools' can also be 'effective schools' and the extent to which educational restructuring and reform are required. The chapter concludes with the need for a more developed definition of 'inclusive schooling' based on principled arguments (derived from consideration of justice and equity) and evaluations of empirical evidence.

## Inclusive schooling and special educational needs

As a term, 'inclusive schooling' has been most closely associated with developments in special educational needs (SEN) (see Chapter 2 for further details). In this context, 'inclusive schooling' relates to the 'inclusion' of pupils designated as having special educational needs into 'mainstream' schools. The term 'inclusion' is being increasingly recognised internationally and perceived as a more positive concept than 'integration' in the UK or 'mainstreaming' in the USA (Clark *et al.*, 1995: v). For example, 'integration' could be interpreted narrowly to imply the physical placement of a pupil into a mainstream school, but not their wider social and educational 'inclusion'. The earlier term 'integration' has been taken to imply that the pupil adapts to the school, whereas the term 'inclusion' implies that the school adapt to meet the needs of all pupils.

As discussed in the introduction, there is no one over-arching definition of 'inclusion'; rather there is a considerable range of interpretations within the SEN literature. As Lunt and Norwich caution: 'there are quite divergent and incompatible concepts of inclusion and … it is a complex concept open to confusion' (1999: 32). This complexity is further explored in Chapter 2. However, in terms of a definition of 'inclusive schooling', it is worth noting that some of the key components include:

- a recognition of individual needs;
- a recognition of individual achievement;
- an appreciation of diversity (as normal and positive rather than as deficit and problematic);
- the physical location of pupils in schools;
- the educational experience of pupils;
- the emotional well-being and social interaction of pupils.

Some key aspects of debate are whether inclusion implies:

- a balance between individual needs and the needs of the majority;
- the active participation of pupils (rather than inclusion being 'done to' them);
- a state of affairs or an ongoing process;
- a relation to exclusion.

As will be discussed in Chapter 2, a particular issue is whether 'inclusive schools for all' requires the 'full inclusion' of all pupils designated as having special educational needs into 'mainstream' settings. There are very strongly held views for both the 'full' inclusion of all pupils or a 'pragmatic' approach which supports inclusion but indicates that there may be a minority of pupils with particularly severe and complex needs requiring specialised support and schools.

## Inclusive schooling and 'all pupils'

With the developing and widening definitions of inclusion associated with the SEN literature, there has been growing debate about the capacity of 'inclusive schools' to meet the needs of all children. For example, Thomas and Loxley argue that:

> The notion of inclusion therefore does not set boundaries (as the notion of integration did) around particular kinds of supposed disability.

Instead, it is about providing a framework within which all children –
regardless of ability, gender, language, ethnic or cultural origin – can be
valued equally, treated with respect and provided with real opportunities
at school. There is the danger, as Slee (1998: 131) has put it, that 'Terms
such as "special educational needs", "integration", "normalisation",
"mainstreaming", "exceptional learners" and "inclusion"… merge into
a loose vocabulary.' That is to say, the terms are bundled together to
represent a single agenda concerning putative learning difficulties and
disability. But inclusion should have a far broader yet more distinct
meaning, moving from what Roaf (1988: 7) has called an 'obsession
with individual learning difficulties' to an agenda of *rights*.

(Thomas and Loxley, 2001: 119, original emphasis)

The need to develop 'inclusive schools' which positively recognise diversity and develop all children has been widely linked to concerns about
human rights and social justice.

Important in this development is the *Salamanca Statement and Framework for Action on Special Needs Education* (UNESCO, 1994), which
was signed by representatives of 92 governments and 25 international
organisations. Although concerned mainly with SEN, the Statement
develops the definition of inclusive schooling as being important to
educational reform for all children in mainstream education.

The principles informing the Statement (UNESCO, 1994: viii) are:

- Every child has a fundamental right to education, and must be given
  the opportunity to achieve and maintain an acceptable level of learning;
- Every child has unique characteristics, interests, abilities and learning
  needs;
- Education systems should be designed and educational programmes
  implemented to take into account the wide diversity of these characteristics and needs;
- Those with special educational needs must have access to regular
  schools which should accommodate them within a child-centred pedagogy capable of meeting these needs;
- Regular schools with this inclusive orientation are the most effective
  means of combating discriminatory attitudes, creating welcoming

communities, building an inclusive society and achieving education for all; moreover, they provide an effective education to the majority of children and improve the efficiency and ultimately the cost-effectiveness of the entire education system.

While these principles of 'inclusive schooling' have been widely promoted and supported internationally, there remains ongoing need for research into the appropriateness, processes and outcomes of inclusive schooling.

The policies associated with these principles advocate widespread reform of schooling, based particularly on a child-centred pedagogy and child-centred schools. The *Salamanca Statement* endorses the fundamental principle that:

> children should learn together, wherever possible, regardless of any difficulties or differences they may have. Inclusive schools must recognize and respond to the diverse needs of their students, accommodating both different styles and rates of learning and ensuring quality education to all through appropriate curricula, organizational arrangements, teaching strategies, resource use and partnerships with their communities. There should be a continuum of support and services to match the continuum of special needs encountered in every school.
>
> (UNESCO, 1994: 11–12)

Recently, the World Health Organisation (WHO) has promoted 'child-friendly schools' to address the educational and psycho-social development of pupils, claiming the following benefits:

> The overall aim is to improve the overall attractiveness of being in school for those who work there and so improve their mental health. At the positive level, the advantages will be in terms of greater well-being, happiness, an improved sense of belonging and better quality of life for all those engaged with the organisation. It can also change some of the more negative aspects of school life, by reducing instances of bullying and harassment, injury, truancy and absenteeism at one level. It can also diminish stereotyping and prejudice, discrimination, fear, anxiety, depression and loss of motivation at another. Furthermore, students

working in a child-friendly environment where they feel a sense of attachment are less likely to vandalise their surroundings, so the community at large may benefit. Long-term, a positive orientation towards school work and the workplace has consequences for adult working life.

(WHO, 1999)

Ainscow (1995: 1) has advocated the creation of 'inclusive schools for all': 'where the aim is to restructure schools in order to respond to the needs of all children'. This argument is based on a conception of human rights and recognition of the multiple and interconnected needs of children, particularly where multiple forms of social disadvantage have implications for educational disadvantage.

*The International Journal of Inclusive Education* (Slee, 1997) offers the following definition, involving an emphasis on pupils who are disadvantaged within society and schooling:

'Inclusive' education extends beyond enrolment to successful participation which generates greater options for all people in education and beyond ... particularly those marginalized, placed 'at risk' by, or excluded from early childhood education, primary and secondary schooling.

However, while 'inclusive' schooling can be perceived as positively encouraging inclusionary processes and reducing exclusionary ones, it has been suggested also that schools themselves may exert, mediate and replicate wider exclusionary processes (Slee, 1997). Thus, Hayton (1999: 171), writing about gender and education, proposes: 'The first step in developing a more inclusive system is a reassessment of some of the basic assumptions that our present system is founded on.' It is suggested that through inclusive schooling and recognition of education's role in promoting inclusion and reducing exclusion, schools can become part of the solution.

In England the Centre for Studies in Inclusive Education (CSIE) has recently produced an *Index for Inclusion* (CSIE, 2000).[1] It proposes the need to consider the range of inclusionary and exclusionary processes and outcomes operating in schools:

Racism, sexism, classism, homophobia, disablism, and bullying all share a common root in an intolerance to difference and the abuse of power to create and perpetuate inequalities. Making schools more inclusive may involve staff in a painful process of challenging their own discriminatory practices and attitudes.

(Booth *et al.*, 2000: 14)

*The Index for Inclusion* promotes a broad definition of 'inclusion' as linked to the needs of all pupils (see Box 1.1). It suggests that there are three key dimensions to an inclusive school: cultures, policies and practices (see Box 1.2). These dimensions are interconnected and, therefore, reform requires addressing all dimensions. The Index provides a tool for schools to reflect on their current inclusive and exclusionary culture, policies and practices and to identify areas for future development.

The need for schools to develop means to counter and reform exclusionary processes and discrimination within schooling has been widely

---

**Box 1.1** *Inclusion in education*

- Inclusion in education involves the processes of increasing the participation of students in, and reducing their exclusion from, the cultures, curricula and communities of local schools.
- Inclusion involves restructuring the cultures, policies and practices in schools so that they respond to the diversity of students in their locality.
- Inclusion is concerned with the learning and participation of all students vulnerable to exclusionary pressures, not only those with impairments or those who are categorised as 'having special educational needs'.
- Inclusion is concerned with improving schools for staff as well as for students.
- A concern with overcoming the barriers to the access and participation of particular students may reveal gaps in the attempts of a school to respond to diversity more generally.
- All students have a right to an education in their locality.
- Diversity is not viewed as a problem to be overcome, but as a rich resource to support the learning of all.
- Inclusion is concerned with fostering mutually sustaining relationships between schools and communities.
- Inclusion in education is one aspect of inclusion in society.

*Source:* Booth *et al.* (2000: 12)

---

**Box 1.2** *Dimensions of inclusive schools*

## Dimension A: Creating inclusive CULTURES

This dimension is about creating a secure, accepting, collaborating, stimulating community in which everyone is valued, as the foundation for the highest achievements of all students. It is concerned with developing inclusive values, shared between all staff, students, governors and parents/carers that are conveyed to all new members of the school. The principles derived within inclusive school cultures guide decisions about policies and moment-to-moment practice so that learning of all is supported through a continuous process of school development.

## Dimension B: Producing inclusive POLICIES

This dimension is about securing inclusion at the heart of school development, permeating all policies, so that they increase the learning and participation of all students. Support is considered as those activities which increase the capacity of a school to respond to student diversity. All forms of support are brought together within a single framework and are viewed from the perspective of students and their development rather than school or local authority administrative structures.

## Dimension C: Evolving inclusive PRACTICES

This dimension is about making school practices reflect the inclusive cultures and policies of the school. It is concerned with ensuring that classroom and extra-curricular activities encourage the participation of all students and draw on their knowledge and experience outside school. Teaching and support are integrated together in the orchestration of learning and the overcoming of barriers to learning and participation. Staff mobilise resources within the school and local communities to sustain active learning for all.

*Source:* Booth *et al.* (2000: 9)

---

advocated. However, there are concerns that a 'broader all-encompassing' definition of discrimination and pupil needs may 'blur and confuse' the need for awareness of particular forms of discrimination and the specific needs of individuals and groups of pupils (Lunt and Norwich, 1999: 30).

While the definitions offered in Boxes 1.1 and 1.2 may contribute towards defining 'inclusive schooling', there is a need for further developments considering both:

• the principled arguments for (and against) inclusion;
• the emerging research evidence concerning exclusionary processes and inclusive practices at school level.

This involves consideration of the different, although sometimes over-lapping, exclusionary processes associated with special educational needs, 'race', gender and social class (these issues are explored in the following chapters). Furthermore, while the Index's conceptualisation of 'barriers to learning and participation' based on a social model rather than per-sonal deficits is important, 'inclusive schooling' must be concerned with reducing barriers and developing strategies which enable learning (see Chapters 6 and 8). The emerging evidence suggests that implementing an idealised notion of 'inclusive schooling' may encounter complications and controversy (see Chapter 2). There is considerable debate about the extent to which 'inclusive schools' are or should also be 'effective schools' (see Chapters 2, 7 and 8). Interwoven with such questions and research evidence are fundamental questions about social justice and equity.

## Social justice and inclusive schooling

The pursuit of social justice has been associated with the developing definitions and scope of 'inclusive schooling' (Lunt and Norwich, 1999). However, in relation to education policy developments and evaluations to date, Gewirtz (1998: 469) contends that there has been 'very little *explicit* discussion of what social justice means or ought to mean'. This is an important point, as social justice is an 'essentially contested concept' (Gallie, 1956) imbued with a range of diverse meanings and associated values (Troyna and Vincent, 1995). It is necessary to consider the various conceptualisations of social justice and their potential relationships to developments in education policy in general and inclusive schooling in particular.

Gewirtz (1998) provides an informed and useful synthesis of the dif-fering definitions and debates associated with social justice. She pro-poses that there are two key dimensions of justice: *distributional justice* and *relational justice*. First, *distributional justice* refers to 'the principles by which goods are distributed in society' (Gewirtz, 1998: 470). This is the classic definition first proposed by Rawls (1972) which is essentially concerned with a 'fair' distribution of material and non-material resources throughout society.

Debates about *equality* have, however, shifted in recent years. The concept of equity has received increasing attention, particularly in the USA, but also developing in the UK. Writing from a USA perspective, Vialli *et al.* comment that:

> equity has replaced the older concept of equal educational opportunity. Both are related to egalitarian concepts of liberty, democracy and freedom from bias (Grant, 1989: 89). But equity places more emphasis on notions of fairness and justice, even if that requires an unequal distribution of goods and services.
>
> (Vialli *et al.*, 1997: 254)

This issue of 'unequal distribution' is contested in developing definitions of equality and equity.

Gillborn and Youdell (2000) propose four key definitions of equality and equity related to education:

1 *Formal equality of access and provision* In its most limited sense, equality of access is concerned with 'formal and explicit barriers to access and participation, such as restrictions on the gender or religion of participants in an organization. Hence, inequality by this definition would rest on members of one or more social or ethnic groups openly being denied access to particular schools or examination systems on the basis of their ascribed identity' (Gillborn and Youdell, 2000: 2; see also Halsey *et al.*, 1980).

2 *Equality of circumstance* 'This perspective is concerned with the inequalities of circumstance that can bar certain groups from participation in practice (especially via poverty) despite the abolition of any formal barrier to access' (Gillborn and Youdell, 2000: 2). Such processes are linked to current concerns about social exclusion and inclusion.

3 *Equity of participation (treatment)* This definition has developed in the USA literature to refer to 'the structures and processes that define everyday life in schools' (Vialli *et al.*, 1997: 254). According to Gillborn

and Youdell, these processes include both the formal and 'hidden' curriculum and inappropriate assessment procedures which 'give structural force to inequalities of "race", gender and class' (2000: 3).

4  *Equity of outcome* This refers to the result of educational processes: the equitable distribution of the benefits of schooling. Equitable outcomes of schooling would decrease, if not eliminate, group differences in school achievement, attendance, exclusions, and post-school transitions (further education and employment) (Vialli *et al.*, 1997: 225).

Gewirtz (1998: 472) proposes that equity of outcome 'seeks to ensure equal rates of success for different groups in society through direct intervention to prevent disadvantage'. This would involve targeted funding and policies and require intervention to advantage those pupils with low educational attainment. Pantazis (2000) suggests that the New Labour government in the UK have emphasised 'equality of opportunity' at the expense of traditional Labour concerns for 'equality of outcome'. She suggests further that this focus on 'opportunity' will not address, and may even exacerbate, inequalities of outcome (Pantazis, 2000).

Consideration of equality and equity issues emphasises the need to distribute goods both to individuals and in terms of social and economic structures. It is not simply about 'who gets what' but also the processes and structures of these relationships. This leads to the second dimension of justice identified by Gewirtz (1998).

*Relational justice* 'refers to the nature of the relationships which structure society' (Gewirtz, 1998: 470–1). It is concerned with power and social relations, for example the daily face-to-face interactions between individuals in classrooms, and wider processes of social and economic structures. While there are various perspectives and definitions of relational justice, of particular importance to the development of inclusive schooling are an emphasis on citizenship, stakeholding and inclusivity. This has been linked also to a focus on 'social capital' which refers to social relationships, networks, shared norms and trust (Putnam, 1995; Vincent, 2000). Of importance also is the concept of 'justice as recognition' (Gewirtz, 1998) which proposes that the different needs of individuals should be recognised, such as those relating to class, gender and 'race', resulting in more appropriate policies reflecting a holistic recognition of individuals' and groups' needs and encouraging their participation and inclusion in development.

Gewirtz (1998) argues that it is important that we are aware of both the distributional and relational dimensions of justice. She contrasts the two approaches, explaining:

> The distributional dimension is essentially individualistic and atomistic, in that it refers to how goods are distributed to individuals in society. In Miller's well-known formulation it means 'ensuring everyone receives their due' (Miller, 1976: 20) By contrast, the relational dimension is holistic and non-atomistic, being essentially concerned with the nature of interconnections between individuals in society, rather than with how much individuals get.
>
> (Gewirtz,1998: 471)

Although there are distinctions between these perspectives, in practice the two dimensions of justice are closely connected.

In developing conceptualisations of social justice (and its relationship to education) Young's (1990) 'five faces of oppression' has been influential. Young argues that we must consider the social injustices resulting from oppression, namely:

1  *exploitation* (for example, in the workplace);
2  *marginalisation* (linked to social exclusionary processes);
3  *powerlessness* (lack of power, authority and respect);
4  *cultural imperialism* (for example, stereotyping or the imposition of a dominant culture on all);
5  *violence* (the fear and event of violent attacks).

Based on this framework, Gewirtz proposed a tentative list of questions relating to education and social justice, asking how, to what extent and why do education policies support, interrupt or subvert:

1  Exploitative relationships (capitalist, patriarchal, racist, homophobic, disabilist, etc.) within and beyond educational institutions?

2 Processes of marginalisation and inclusion within and beyond the education system?

3 The promotion of relationships based on recognition, respect, care and mutuality or which produce powerlessness (for education workers and students)?

4 Practices of cultural imperialism, and which cultural differences should be affirmed, which should be universalised and which rejected?

5 Violent practices within and beyond the education system?

(Gewirtz, 1998: 482)

Although there is debate about the extent to which education can and/or should promote social justice and ameliorate social injustices, there is a growing reform movement proposing that education is 'one of the main arenas for the promotion of social justice' (Troyna and Vincent, 1995: 152). Within the UK, prominent policies for promoting social justice ideals have included the development of comprehensive education, mixed ability teaching, provision for pupils with special educational needs, anti-racist and multicultural education and anti-sexist initiatives (see Troyna and Vincent, 1995). More recently, policies aimed at reducing social exclusion and enhancing social inclusion have been associated with the pursuit of social justice. Indeed, some advocates of inclusive schooling would consider its role in promoting social justice as an educational, political and moral imperative (see for example, Armstrong *et al.*, 2000; Corbett and Slee, 2000).

## Social exclusion

The term 'social exclusion' has developed considerably over time and within different national contexts (see for example: Sostris, 1997; Cousins, 1998; Parsons, 1999; Percy-Smith, 2000). In recent years, a focus on 'social exclusion' (and even more recently 'social inclusion') has become widespread across Europe.

Research has sought to illuminate the different definitions of 'social exclusion' in order to reveal commonalities and tensions between different national approaches. Chamberlayne (1997) indicates that there are considerable differences in the meaning and interpretation of 'social exclusion' and its embodiment in policy and research between different countries in Europe. Cousins (1998) suggests that these differences can be understood in terms of four differing 'paradigms of social exclusion and inclusion':

1  *The 'solidarity' paradigm* emphasises the linkage between an individual and society. When this linkage is weakened or broken, social exclusionary processes occur. Therefore, there is a concern with social inclusion, citizenship and civil rights.
2  *The 'specialisation' paradigm* focuses on individual differences within market economies and social groupings. Exclusionary processes are associated with discrimination, lack of rights and economic inequalities.
3  *The 'monopoly' paradigm* relates exclusion and inequality to the outcome of group monopolies, linked particularly to class and power, resulting in the subordination of specific groups. Hence, there is a need to consider issues of citizenship and participation.
4  *An 'organic' paradigm* focuses on group processes for social integration and inclusion. It advocates that groups should be formed around local communities emphasising harmonious relationships, rather than class, religious, ethnic or other divisions.

While specific forms of these paradigms have been influential in particular countries and policies, in practice the paradigms do not relate specifically and exclusively to national boundaries.

Leney (1999) proposes that along with an increasing interest in the European Commission and European Union about social exclusion and inclusion, there has been some convergence of definitions (although other writers, for example Sostris, 1997, would disagree). Concerns about 'social exclusion' are also related both to distributional dimensions (e.g. poverty) and relational dimensions (e.g. participation in society). Therefore, although issues of poverty and disadvantage are frequently central to current discussions of exclusion, 'social exclusion' as a concept and process is broader. As Leney (1999: 35) explains:

- *Poverty* is defined as an absolute or relative lack of material resources, particularly income, and the policy solution usually proposed is the provision of an adequate minimum income, whether through employment or benefit;
- *Deprivation* is defined as a lack of material standards, services and amenities, and the policy solution envisaged in this scenario is usually to provide adequate minimum standards of living that include income, services (including education and training) and amenities;
- *Social exclusion* is given a more complex definition: the process of being detached from the organizations and communities that compose society, and from the rights and obligations (which are economic, social, political, cultural and educational) of mainstream society. Policy solutions include both providing access to employment, income, adequate housing and education, training and other resources and developing processes that create and reinforce forms of social inclusion, such as family support and common citizenship, social capital (hence the emphasis on education and training) and regenerating local communities.

The multi-dimensional nature of social exclusion and inclusion is recognised and requires ongoing investigation (see for example, Burchardt *et al.*, 1999; Percy-Smith, 2000). As Leney cautions:

> it is possible that social exclusion theories and policies run a risk of becoming reductionist – either by falling back into a version of reproduction theory or by pathologizing individuals or specific social groups. The challenge is to develop an analysis that links the changing social structures of advantage/disadvantage with the mechanisms and networks that operate ... and which can also engage with trajectories and feelings of the individuals or groups involved.
>
> (Leney, 1999: 37)

He argues that analysis which explores linkages between social structures and inequalities, social relationships and networks and the 'experiences of people as they experience a range of transitions' will develop research and policy (Leney, 1999: 38).

Leney (1999) points to the creation by the European Commission of the European Observatory on Policies to Combat Social Exclusion in 1990 as important. Since 1995, the European Commission has promoted developments for an 'inclusive learning society' and 'inclusive education' (European Commission, 1995). Although the European Commission cannot directly mandate change in national education systems, Leney (1999: 41–3) points to a number of common developments among European Union member states:

- providing access for all to pre-school education;
- providing common opportunities for access to a wide range of knowledge and a growing range of skills during the phases of compulsory education;
- making provision for a high proportion of each cohort to continue into post-compulsory education and training, which means that the end of compulsory education marks the end of schooling for fewer and fewer young people;
- opening up constructive opportunities for the 10 to 20 per cent of young people who leave formal education or training with few or no qualifications;
- improving the quality and raising the status of vocational education and training (VET), and tackling the status differential between general education and VET (including apprenticeships);
- recognising skills gained through other means than formal qualification, and establishing ways of achieving more flexible access to both higher education and lifelong learning.

However, for the purposes of this review, it should be noted that the above developments relate mostly to transitions and developments pre and post compulsory schooling.

The creation of the Social Exclusion Unit in the UK Cabinet Office in 1997 has been perceived as pivotal. The SEU has emphasised that social exclusion is a 'joined up' problem requiring 'joined up' solutions. The goals of the SEU include preventing social exclusion, reintegrating those who are excluded from society and 'getting the basics right' in terms of providing access to employment, an adequate income, health and education (SEU, 2001). In relation to schools specifically, three key areas for improvement were identified early on: exclusion from school, truancy and teenage pregnancy. Policy developments and some improvements in all these areas have occurred (see SEU, 2001).

The linkages between *school* exclusion specifically and wider processes of social exclusion have been particularly debated by researchers. For example, Blyth and Milner asked whether 'exclusion from school' was 'a first step in exclusion from society' (1993: 255). This raises important questions around rights and justice. More recent analyses have explored the complex processes and issues surrounding school exclusion and their relationship to social exclusion. Parsons (1999) argues there are three broad sets of exclusionary and inclusionary processes which impact on an individual's propensity to be excluded from school; these relate to socio-economic and cultural factors, institutional (school-level) factors and individual factors. Of these, he argues that socio-economic and cultural factors are the most important but also the most difficult to reform, particularly through direct educational policies.

According to Parsons (1999), we must recognise that school exclusion takes place within (and may contribute to) a wider context of social exclusionary processes and outcomes. The relationship between school exclusion and social exclusion requires ongoing research. However, it should be noted that rates of exclusion (expulsion) from school can vary dramatically between different schools and localities over time. For example, the dramatic increase in school exclusion in England and Wales in the 1990s highlights the vital importance of school-based factors and policy consequences.[2]

## Inclusive societies and schools

The link between inclusive schooling and inclusive societies is also pertinent to this review. Many advocates of inclusive schooling perceive it as being a component of wider social inclusion and the reduction of exclusion. For example the Salamanca Statement proposed that:

The merit of such [inclusive] schools is not only that they are capable of providing quality education to all children; their establishment is a crucial step in helping to change discriminatory attitudes, in creating welcoming communities and in developing an inclusive society. A change in social perspective is imperative.

(UNESCO, 1994: 6–7)

Evidence suggests that some schools can demonstrate success in developing more inclusive processes and practices and in enabling pupils from disadvantaged backgrounds to achieve academic improvements (see Chapter 7). However, there is considerable debate about the extent to which schools can 'compensate' for society and ameliorate inequitable social and cultural structures and the multiple forms of disadvantage which impact on pupils (Bernstein, 1970).

There has been considerable debate as to the balance between 'school effects' (associated with school effectiveness and school improvement literatures) and wider social and economic inequalities (associated with sociological interpretations) on pupils' performance in school. Mortimore and Whitty (1997, 1999) highlight the deep-rooted and multiple causes of social disadvantage in the UK. They note with concern that indicators of social disadvantage affecting children demonstrate a considerable worsening of conditions in the contemporary UK during the 1980s to mid-1990s (as discussed also in the Introduction and see Pantazis, 2000).[3] Mortimore and Whitty note also the ongoing evidence indicating that social disadvantage impacts on educational outcomes, stating that 'There is a strong negative correlation between most measures of social disadvantage and school achievement' (1999: 80).

Mortimore and Whitty (1999) suggest that many previous 'remedies' for social and educational disadvantage have been problematic. For example, an emphasis on meritocracy, associated with selection and often embodied in examination procedures, has had mixed outcomes. While it may benefit a specific minority of individuals, it has failed to benefit the majority of disadvantaged students.

Compensatory approaches have differing impacts also. Compensations aimed at individuals from low income backgrounds (e.g. free school meals) can be important but are limited in the levels of funding involved and the extent to which they can have a widespread impact on educational processes and outcomes. Compensatory measures targeted at the school level can create improvements. However, depending on eligibility and funding mechanisms, these improvements may also benefit non-disadvantaged pupils in the targeted schools, while leaving disadvantaged pupils in non-targeted schools with no additional support. The key point is whether funding is targeted to specific schools or whether funding is targeted to the needs of individual pupils across schools (Sammons *et al.*, 1997). As noted throughout this book, specific local intervention projects can have positive effects and are locally supported. However, without national support for policy development and implementation, local strategies cannot be implemented more widely.

Since the late 1990s, there has been an emphasis on school effectiveness and school improvement strategies (see Chapter 7). This research has indicated a range of practices and processes relating to within-school factors that can impact on the effectiveness of schools. Some schools have been particularly successful in developing school improvement strategies and effectiveness in 'adding value' to the progress of pupils. However, critics have urged caution in expecting all schools to be capable of improving at the same rate and to the same extent (see for example, Ouston, 1999).

Furthermore, if all schools did improve at the same rate, there are concerns that even with improvements in all pupils' performance, the social stratification of educational attainment would remain essentially intact. Although there may be an *absolute* improvement in overall attainment levels and educational performance, attention needs to be paid to *relative* improvements in the attainment of different groups of students, as Gillborn and Gipp's (1996) analyses of 'race', gender and social class revealed in England (see also Hatcher, 1998; Gillborn and Mirza, 2000). As discussed in Chapter 7, school effectiveness research is concerned with 'differential effectiveness', exploring the processes and outcomes of schooling for different individuals and groups of students. There is a need to be aware of the extent to which social inequalities can impact on processes within schooling, requiring attention to be paid, for example, to curriculum and assessment (Mortimore and Whitty, 1997, 1999).

Developing links between inclusive schooling and social inclusion requires multiple policies creating reform at school and societal levels. As Mortimore and Whitty explain:

> What we have been concerned to stress ... is that society needs to be clearer about what schools can and cannot be expected to do. The relationship between individuals, institutions and society is complex and blaming schools for the problems of society is unfair and unproductive.
>
> (Mortimore and Whitty, 1999: 90)

This is not to say that 'school effects' are unimportant or that schools do not make a difference. However, the linkages between educational reform and other social and economic reforms must be emphasised, creating 'joined up solutions'. In this context, 'if dynamic school improvement strategies can be developed as one aspect of a broader social policy, then they will have an important role to play' (Mortimore and Whitty, 1999: 90). Within education, Mortimore and Whitty (1999: 90) advocate the following strategies for reducing social exclusion and promoting school improvements:

- better co-ordination of the work of the support agencies by the government and by local authorities;
- early interventions that provide additional educational opportunities for the disadvantaged, funded from an increased education budget;
- reconsideration of the approaches to learning and teaching used with disadvantaged students;
- extra support for students with disadvantaged backgrounds in school improvement programmes.

In the development of inclusive processes, as this book emphasises, there is a need to consider both the policies and practices in schooling *and* to consider linkages with parents/carers, families, communities and other agencies.

## Inclusive and effective schools

In developing inclusive schools, there is considerable debate as to whether 'inclusive schools' can also be 'effective schools' (see for example: Lunt and Norwich, 1999; Rouse and Florian, 1996; Sebba and Ainscow, 1996). There have been concerns that popular perceptions of school 'effectiveness' have centred on narrow measures of educational attainment, as evident in 'league tables' (Ouston, 1999). It is suggested that the policy emphasis on both raising academic attainment and promoting school inclusion (and reducing school exclusion) may create tensions (Parsons, 1999) and may even be contradictory (Gillborn and Youdell, 2000). However, as discussed in Chapter 7, school effectiveness research (SER) is critical of raw league tables measures. Although school effectiveness is concerned with outcomes, SER stresses pupil progress also and the 'value added' by schools, particularly for children 'at risk' of educational underachievement. Questions have been raised as to whether schools which meet the needs of pupils with special educational needs are also effective at meeting the needs of all pupils (Lunt and Norwich, 1999). There have, therefore, been debates about the 'effectiveness' of schools for specific groups of pupils and for all pupils.

Some researchers propose that the development of 'effective inclusive' schools is crucial. For example, Sebba and Ainscow offer the following definition:

> Inclusion describes the process by which a school attempts to respond to all pupils as individuals by reconsidering its curricular organisation and provision. Through this process, the school builds its capacity to accept all pupils from the local community who wish to attend and, in so doing, reduces the need to exclude pupils.
>
> (Sebba and Ainscow, 1996: 9)

They suggest this definition requires the interconnection of inclusive schooling and school effectiveness. Rouse and Florian propose that:

> effective inclusive schools are diverse problem solving organisations with a common mission that emphasises learning for all students. They

employ and support teachers and other staff who are committed to working together to create and maintain a climate conducive to learning. The responsibility for all students is shared. Effective inclusive schools acknowledge that such a commitment requires clear policies, administrative leadership and long-term professional development.

Because schools are diverse, dynamic places, each having its own history and culture, there are different ways of achieving effective inclusive schools. Moreover, what works in one community may not be effective in another. One factor, however, seems to be constant, and that is the need for long-term professional development for all the adults involved. Such staff development needs to address issues of collaboration, team building, problem solving, evaluation, assessment and curriculum ... What is most important is that any planning must involve all the stakeholders in the school as well as representatives of the community.

(Rouse and Florian, 1996: 83)

For these researchers, inclusive schools should also be effective schools.

Nevertheless, there is ongoing debate about the features of 'inclusive schools', 'effective schools' and 'inclusive effective schools', for example linked to the development of universal reform strategies versus reforms targeted in an attempt to ameliorate inequalities and social disadvantage (Hatcher, 1998; Mortimore and Whitty, 1999). There is debate about the extent to which organisational and managerial reforms at school level (as advocated in school effectiveness and school improvement literatures) can lead to significant developments in inclusionary processes and improvements (Ouston, 1999). As discussed in Chapter 7, 'effectiveness' is a relative concept and schools may demonstrate differing levels of 'effectiveness', requiring examination of: which outcomes schools are effective in promoting (the *what* of effectiveness); effective for which student groups (the *who* of effectiveness); and effective over what time period (the *when* of effectiveness). Some advocates of inclusive schooling would argue the need for a more radical agenda creating fundamental changes throughout the education system, for example in policies, structures and cultures (see for example, Corbett and Slee, 2000).

## Inclusive schools as reformed schools

Throughout this book, it is suggested that the development of inclusive schooling requires building on existing evidence of good practice and further reform of schools. The concept of 'inclusive schooling' has been widely debated and various models have been proposed. Such models recognise links between the processes in schools with the wider involvement of families, communities and other agencies in generating inclusive schooling (see for example: Boscardin and Jacobson, 1996; Sailor, 1996; Sailor *et al.*, 1996).

For example, Boscardin and Jacobson (1996) propose an ideal model of inclusive schooling that involves reconsidering the structure and purpose of schooling. They suggest that, structurally, inclusive schools should be perceived as locally-based communities, with an emphasis on shared values and local participation. They should have a common purpose to develop and promote 'inclusive schooling', based on a positive recognition of and respect for the diverse needs of their pupils and local communities.

Writing in the USA from a SEN perspective, Sailor and colleagues adopted the term 'New Community Schools' to promote reform which creates change for children and families. They suggest that three interlinked reform processes are central and that the key ingredients of public policy transformations that make up the New Community School concept are (see also Sailor *et al.*, 1996):

1  *School-linked services integration:* A school–community partnership arrangement that addresses human support needs in a broader social context and that is consumer rather than agency empowering.

2  *School restructuring:* General education reform processes that utilize the collective strengths of school staff through collaborative planning and governance structures, to better address the needs of all students.

3  *Inclusive education:* Reform processes in special education that apply the specialized supports and technology of that discipline in an integrated context that enhances the education of all students at the school while supporting specific students in the mainstream of general education.

(Sailor, 1996: 199)

Moss *et al.* (1999) suggest that 'school inclusion' requires 'rethinking' schools, including their purpose and structure, and 'rethinking' the nature of childhood and pupils. However, while the above models proposed by Boscardin and Jacobson (1996) and Sailor (1996) offer principles and proposals for reform, they are essentially idealised.

## Reviewing inclusive schooling

The above discussion of the definitions and dimensions of inclusive schooling reveal that there is no one definition of inclusive schooling. As explained from the outset, defining 'inclusive schooling' is complex and contested. A range of definitions and issues derived from a wider consideration of social justice, equity and social exclusion are considered. There are potential tensions between promoting inclusion for all and the need to recognise the individual needs of disadvantaged and discriminated groups of pupils. There is a need also for careful consideration of the association between social processes and outcomes and those in and through schooling. The movement towards 'inclusive schooling' requires consideration of both principled and empirical arguments and evidence. To review developments in inclusive schooling, there is need for 'a knowledge-base generated by inquiry such that particular practices and propositions have demonstrable grounding' (Clark *et al.*, 1995: 166).

## Notes

1  In collaboration with the Centre for Educational Needs, University of Manchester, and the Centre for Educational Research, Canterbury Christ Church University College.
2  An increase of 400 per cent between 1990 and 1996.
3  For example, they refer to figures published in 1997 indicating that 32 per cent of children in the UK live in poor households compared to a European average of 32 per cent (Eurostat, 1997).

# 2 The challenge of inclusive schooling for pupils with special educational needs

*Ingrid Lunt*

The notion of 'inclusive schooling' is complex in relation to students designated as having special educational needs or disabilities. There is no one definition of what 'inclusive schooling' would entail, nor is there universal agreement that 'one school for all' is the most appropriate means to meet all students' individual needs. Although all would agree that most children designated as having special educational needs should be educated in mainstream schools, this may be debatable for a small minority of children with severe and complex needs whose education some consider may be more appropriately organised in specialised schools. The question therefore arises whether 'inclusive' schools should be expected to provide for all the pupils of a local community, or whether there may be a very small number of individuals for whom mainstream schools may not be appropriate, or not for all the time, and who may have a right to an alternative form of education. This question is extremely complex and there are strongly held views on both sides. In addition, in relation to pupils designated as having special educational needs, there is a need to balance the needs of individuals with the needs of the majority. In this chapter, I trace the legislation and the development of concepts in relation to this field, before considering issues such as school choice, contradictory values and the issue of rights, issues of resourcing, and some outcome evaluation studies. Finally I present some strategies and aspects of inclusive schools and schooling which have proved promising.

## Legislation

Coinciding with wider moves towards human rights, equal opportunities and 'normalisation' (Wolfensberger, 1972), legislation in relation to pupils with disabilities was passed in most so-called developed countries during the 1970s and 1980s (e.g. US PL-142, (Public Law) the Education for all Handicapped Children Act; UK the 1981 Education Act) (OECD, 1995; UNESCO, 1988, 1995; Daniels and Garner, 1999; Mittler, 2000). This legislation provided in most countries for the greater 'integration' of all pupils into mainstream schools or 'mainstreaming'. The nature of the legislation varied considerably between countries; in some countries legislation was more prescriptive, while in others it was enabling rather than prescriptive (OECD, 1995; and see Meijer *et al.*, 1994; Pijl *et al.*, 1997; and see Daniels and Garner, 1999). Within the past decade the term 'integration' has been replaced by the term 'inclusion', which both implies a significant shift in conceptualisation and practice and has also become the term used internationally.

The movement for *full inclusion* is part of a more recent human rights agenda including the UN Convention on the Rights of the Child (1989), the UN Standard Rules on the Equalisation of Opportunities for Persons with Disabilities (1993) and the UNESCO *Salamanca Statement* (1994), and more specific statements such as that of the Centre for Study in Inclusive Education in the UK (CSIE, 1996). However, there are quite divergent views as to what is meant by 'inclusion' (e.g. Lunt and Norwich, 1999: 32) and the realisation of a commitment to 'inclusion' is by no means straightforward.

Within England and Wales the 1981 Education Act followed the Warnock Report (DES, 1978) and was enabling rather than prescriptive. It contained a number of provisos, such as 'efficient use of resources', which led to a qualified or conditional form of integration, and enabled local education authorities (LEAs) to continue to justify segregated provision. These have been retained by current legislation (1993 and 1996 Education Acts) and government documents such as the Code of Practice for SEN (DfE, 1994), the government Green Paper (DfEE, 1997a) which asserts the right of the pupil with SEN to be educated in mainstream schools 'wherever possible', and the Programme of Action (DfEE, 1998a) which promotes inclusion 'where parents want it and where appropriate support can be provided'. Similarly, more recent legislation in the US – the 1990 Individuals with Disabilities Education Act (IDEA) and its Reauthorization (1997) – while guaranteeing to all students with disabilities 'a free appropriate education' in the 'least restrictive environment', also supports the continued existence of a continuum of provision including special schools (Yell, 1998).

It has been pointed out that recent legislative changes have seen a 'shift from legislation and policies based upon principles of equity, social progress and altruism, to new legislation underpinned by a market-place philosophy based on principles of academic excellence, choice and competition' (Rouse and Florian, 1997: 324; and see Evans and Lunt, 1994; Lloyd, 2000). These authors point out a number of tensions between principles underpinning the market-based reforms and those that underpin the development of inclusive education. These tensions are also evident in other European countries and the USA.

Strong impetus to the idea of inclusive education was provided by the UNESCO World Conference on Special Needs Education in Salamanca in 1994 (UNESCO, 1994), which has influenced policy across the world. The *Salamanca Statement*, as mentioned in Chapter 1, proposes that the development of schools with an 'inclusive' orientation is the most effective and efficient means of improving the entire education system; this statement has had a major impact on policies throughout the world

Although there are differences in interpretation of the concept of 'inclusion', the principle of inclusion is no longer in question. While practice within and between countries is extremely varied, the idea that students designated as having disabilities and learning difficulties should in principle be educated alongside their peers in regular schools, wherever possible and appropriate, is no longer seriously questioned in education discourse in most western countries (Hegarty, 1998; and see Meijer *et al.*, 1994; Mittler, 2000). Nevertheless, as mentioned above, considerations of inclusion in practice lead to widely differing views, ranging from those who aspire to total inclusion on ideological and principled grounds (e.g. Thomas, 1997; Booth, 2000) to those who see limits to inclusion on grounds of individual choice, need and practical organisation (e.g. O'Brien, 2001). Contrasts have been drawn between inclusion as a 'never ending process' (Ainscow, 1999; Booth, 2000) involving a radical reform of the school, and inclusion as simply the placement of pupils with disabilities in mainstream schools.

## Concepts of disability

Implementation of the legislation of the 1970s and 1980s in major countries across the world led to new conceptualisations of and approaches to disability in terms of more contextualised, relative and interactive notions, such as 'special educational needs' or 'learning difficulties' in the UK (e.g. Norwich, 1990; Wedell, 1993). However, the issue of categorisation of disability is a major dilemma in the provision of appropriate education for all pupils. Although England and Wales were the only countries to formally abandon categories of handicap or disability (in the 1981 Act), these became replaced by less precise categories such as 'learning difficulties' (Norwich, 1990) and continue to be enshrined both in practice and in policy documents such as the Code of Practice despite their problematic nature (Norwich, 1999; Farrell, 2001). In the US, Public Law 94-142 includes eleven different classifications of handicapping conditions, while most other countries have retained some form of categories of disability for purposes of assessment, provision of services and monitoring of provision (e.g. the Netherlands retains fourteen categories). Indeed there has been a concern that rights of students could be reduced if category labels were eliminated for students with disabilities (Reynolds *et al.*, 1987).

   In the US, the concept of 'least restrictive environment' (LRE) was introduced in 1974 by PL 94-142. This concept has not been without controversy with a view that a preoccupation with LRE has distracted attention away from the key issue of individually appropriate instruction (e.g. Crockett and Kauffman, 1999), and focused on placement rather than a curriculum to optimise learning outcomes. In the UK the shift in conceptualisation of children's needs from individual handicap to 'special educational need' led to a shift in focus from the child to the school, and to an examination of ways in which schools could better meet a wider range of pupils' needs. The term 'integration', used in the 1980s (whether this means 'locational', 'social' or 'functional' as described in the Warnock Report (DES, 1978)) became seen to imply a narrow view of 'placement' of the individual child, or an assumption that the child adapt to the system. Indeed, 'LRE' has been criticised as assuming a 'readiness' model: i.e. pupils must demonstrate their readiness for integrated settings (Lipsky and Gartner, 1996), as opposed to schools demonstrating their readiness to meet the needs of all pupils.

Thus the shift to the term 'inclusion' implies a major shift in conceptualisation (Thomas *et al.*, 1998; Ainscow 1997, 1998; Mittler, 2000). Although there are divergent and contradictory concepts of 'inclusion', the concept does imply that the school adapt to meet as wide a range of pupil diversity as possible. At the same time, there has been a move from the language of 'handicap' (deficit) to a discourse of 'need' (still deficit) and then to the discourse of rights and entitlement (e.g. Roaf and Bines, 1989; Clough, 1998), or a move from a 'within-child' model to a social model of disability. A number of commentators declare the rights of all children to be educated in their mainstream neighbourhood school (e.g. Barton, 1997; Oliver, 1996). This orientation on rights places the responsibility for adjustment on the ordinary school (and see Mittler, 2000).

The shift from 'integration' to 'inclusion' has led to concepts of 'inclusive schools for all' (Ainscow, 1998), the notion of 'inclusive culture' (Corbett, 1999), and inclusive education as 'an unending process' (Booth, 2000). In the US, movements developed such as the 'regular education initiative' (which had as its goal the merging of special and general education into a single organisational structure with all pupils educated in regular school) and the 'inclusive schooling' movement (Stainback and Stainback, 1989; Fuchs and Fuchs, 1994). A review of two decades' experience of PL 94-142 in the US called for a complete change and reconceptualisation of the educational system in order to achieve a 'restructured unitary system' (Gartner and Lipsky, 1987; and see Lipsky and Gartner, 1996). In England the *Index for Inclusion* (CSIE, 2000) and a number of studies have attempted to identify key features of inclusive schools, while Newham Education Authority has made a policy commitment to 'full inclusion' (Jordan and Goodey, 1996).

However, these developments have to be seen alongside a growing number of commentators putting forward more cautious approaches. For example Low suggests that 'the quest for full inclusion contains a measure of expressive zeal which denies some of the realities of disability' and calls for a model 'which recognizes that disabled people are in fundamental respects, at one and the same time, both the same as and different from non-disabled people' (Low 1997: 78).

Others point out the contradictory elements in thinking and discourse between a principled and ideological stand towards inclusion compared with a more pragmatic orientation (Skidmore, 1999; Croll and Moses, 2000a). In the US, there has been a growing criticism of what is perceived by some to be a blind move to full inclusion, informed by ideological rather than pedagogical considerations (Kauffman and Hallahan, 1995; Borthwick-Duffy *et al.*, 1996), and which focus on placement in mainstream at all costs rather than providing the most appropriate curriculum and environment to optimise learning outcomes for each pupil.

This has led some to call for the replacement of the rhetoric of full inclusion with the promotion of 'responsible inclusion' (Vaughn and Schumm, 1995; Hornby, 1999), while in the USA 'cautious inclusivists' point out that the needs of individual pupils are in danger of being neglected with the move to 'full inclusion' (e.g. Kauffman, 1995; Fuchs and Fuchs, 1994). Others point out 'the very real difficulties one can get into if arguments about inclusive education are pursued solely in terms of human rights' (Farrell, 2000: 155; and see Wilson 1999, 2000).

It is evident therefore, that the concept of 'inclusion' of pupils designated as having disabilities or SEN is highly complex and controversial. While on the one hand principles of social justice demand that all students with disabilities be educated in mainstream settings, on the other hand policies need to be supported by evidence that pupils' individual needs are being met (and see Rizvi and Lingard, 1996).

## Choice

The concept of consumer choice is a fundamental principle in many western countries (see Mitchell, 1996; Whitty, 1997). Thus a major issue for education continues to be whether to maintain a unitary system ('one school for all' as in Denmark and Norway, for example), or a dual system with special provision in parallel with mainstream schools.

The authors of the government Green Paper in England and Wales see a continued role for special schools, stating that parents 'continue to have a right to express a preference for a special school where they consider this appropriate to their child's needs' (DfEE, 1997a). Further, the Programme of Action of England and Wales aims to promote 'inclusion within mainstream where parents want it and appropriate support can be provided' (DfEE, 1998a: 23), while stating a continued commitment to develop the role of special schools.

There is abundant evidence that parents wish to maintain their right to choose the school which they consider meets the needs of their child, and many continue to press for a special school place for their child. Some parents choose special schools in the belief that this will protect resources for their children, while others prefer to have their children educated with children with similar difficulties and with access to highly specialist provision. Indeed, as shown by some cases that reach the Tribunal in England and Wales (established by the 1993 Education Act to deal with appeals against assessment and placement decisions) there is a growing number of parents of children with disorders such as autistic spectrum disorder, dyslexia or hearing impairment who fight for specialist provision (often in a special school) for their children. In most countries it appears to be necessary to maintain a dual system of mainstream support and special provision outside the mainstream (Fish and Evans, 1995).

In 1992 the Audit Commission found in England and Wales that inclusion was being held back both by the financing of support and by the fact that resources held in separate special schools had not been transferred to mainstream schools (Audit Commission/HMI, 1992). It was suggested that there is a financial disincentive for authorities to move pupils from special schools to mainstream schools as they then have to fund the ordinary school place as well as the empty special school place. Unless funding policies support inclusion with adequate resources and a transfer of funds with the pupils, this will continue to limit possibilities for inclusive schooling. There is a more fundamental question as to whether the principles of inclusion and choice can be compatible principles (Riddell, 2000).

The maintenance of a dual system of education with separate special schools ensures that parents of pupils designated as having learning difficulties are able to choose mainstream or special provision for their child. Nevertheless, the existence of two separate systems means that it is difficult to shift resources from special provision to mainstream support. Further it could be suggested that the availability of special school placements means that mainstream schools do not need to change to meet the full diversity of pupils' needs, since placement in a special school is always an option. Since the decisions of the Tribunal are binding on LEAs, parental choice of special school, regardless of LEA policies or resources, means that LEAs are obliged to provide the special placement.

## Values and rights

The field of special needs education demands the balancing of multiple values such as the values of equality, of individuality, of social inclusion and of practicability (Norwich, 1996). As already mentioned, there is a tension between those who regard 'the move to inclusion [a]s a principled one' (Thomas, 1997) and those who take a more pragmatic stance, reflecting a tension between pupils' rights to inclusion and their rights to appropriate education and individually relevant learning.

For some, inclusion is seen as a general social and political value and as a matter of civil or human rights: 'segregation in education is a contravention of human rights as is segregation because of race or gender' (CSIE, 1989: 2). Others, for example Low (1997: 78), suggest that 'the question whether services are better provided in the mainstream or separately is a pragmatic one, rather than one of principle'.

The debate over the meaning of 'inclusion' becomes polarised in the question of an individual's basic human right to be educated in the neighbourhood school (e.g. Oliver, 1996) as opposed to their right to an appropriate education to meet their needs (Lindsay, 1997; Hornby, 1999; Farrell, 2000). There are those such as Wilson (1999) who points out the tension between what he refers to as 'ideology' and 'logic', and suggests that the question 'what sorts of learning activities actually suit what types of pupils?' is more appropriate than the attempt to make one school fit all pupils. Indeed much of the discourse on 'inclusion' ignores curricular issues and what actually happens in the classroom; although the National Curriculum was intended to be an 'entitlement curriculum', there are major questions of its operationalisation and differentiation of the curriculum in the mainstream classroom. There is a more general question of the balance of interests and rights between majorities and minorities, and of the rights of all individuals to optimise their learning. This relates to notions of sameness and difference, and the dilemma of whether to identify individual needs and risk stigma, or not to identify and risk losing protected provision.

Inclusive schooling involves contradictory rights and values. There may be tensions between the rights of the majority and the minority, and between an individual pupil's rights to participate and his or her rights to an individually relevant education. Commentators are divided as to whether inclusion is a matter of human rights and a social and political issue, or whether a more pragmatic and flexible approach to meeting individual needs is more appropriate.

## Where are students educated?

Despite legislative commitments to educate students with disabilities in mainstream schools, the move towards greater inclusion has been slow in most countries. What has happened in most countries over the past twenty years is that more pupils have been identified (in mainstream schools) as having disabilities or special educational needs, and an increasing proportion of the education budget is allocated to them. Lipsky and Gartner (1996) point out that since PL 94-142 in 1975, the placement pattern has remained nearly identical in the US with one-third of pupils with disabilities in regular classes, one-third in resource rooms and one-third in special classes and more restrictive settings. The majority of pupils with disabilities are still segregated to an extent (Lipsky and Gartner, 1998).

In England and Wales the percentage of pupils in special schools has fallen from 2 per cent in 1978 to 1.35 per cent in 1998 (Norwich, 1997, 2000). Thus, despite the push for integration, in many western countries a substantial number of students with disabilities remain in segregated settings (Jenkinson, 1997). Quoting from the 1995 OECD study of integration, Hegarty (1998) demonstrates that the European countries range from 0.60 (Norway) to 3.63 (Netherlands) in the percentage of pupils educated in special schools or units, but that these figures conceal enormous diversity of practice across Europe. However, such comparisons need to be used with caution because of differences in the ways in which countries collect statistics, describe pupils' needs and assign different kinds of provision. Nevertheless, reviewing data from eight European countries, Pijl and Meijer conclude that 'the countries seem to agree that at least 1.5 per cent of the students are difficult to integrate on a curricular level in regular education' (1991: 111).

Although England and Wales abolished official categories of handicap in the 1981 Act, other countries have retained categories of handicap as a way of identifying need and allocating resources. In England and Wales in effect a new form of broader categorisation was introduced (different forms of 'learning difficulties' which are defined formally in the *Code of Practice* (DfE 1994)). The statistics from England and Wales conceal differences in the types of pupils who are included, with greater inclusion of pupils with physical and sensory difficulties (Farrell and Mittler, 1998), while those with severe and profound difficulties remain in segregated provision. There appears to be an increase in the number of pupils with Down's syndrome who are educated in mainstream schools, at least at primary level (Cuckle, 1997; Cunningham *et al.*, 1998).

## Inclusion and exclusion

A number of commentators have argued for the need to see inclusion as a process alongside exclusion (Booth and Ainscow, 1998; Parsons, 1999), in particular the exclusion of pupils whose behaviour causes concern and who become known as pupils with emotional and behavioural difficulties. The fact that 'inclusion' usually refers to pupils with learning difficulties, while exclusion is commonly applied to those whose behaviour causes concern, masks the need for wider organisational responses to the full range of diversity. With market-oriented policies and a competitive environment where governments are concerned with standards, 'league' tables and narrowly defined academic performance, in many countries there has been an increase in the number of young people whom schools find difficult to include and who, in countries where exclusion from school is permitted, are excluded from school (Parsons and Howlett, 1996). Indeed, in many countries pupils whose behaviour causes concern (frequently known as pupils with emotional and behavioural difficulties) are found to be the most difficult to include in mainstream schools. However, it may not be appropriate to consider these pupils to have disabilities, but in many cases rather to view their behaviour as a reaction to circumstances or a response to an inappropriate curriculum. As Parsons and Howlett point out 'educational resources are stretched: schools, acting as small businesses, experience the tension between the business ethic and the professional ethic. Where the former prevails they may be encouraged to exclude those who impede the productive/commercial enterprise' (1996: 112).

Thus, despite widespread commitment to educating pupils with learning disabilities in mainstream schools, in most western countries there remain a small number of pupils whose needs are difficult to meet in mainstream, and who continue to be educated in special schools. While a number of commentators question whether mainstream schools are able to meet the needs of pupils with profound and multiple difficulties, the rise in the number of pupils excluded from school on the grounds of their behaviour highlights another group of pupils whose needs schools find it difficult to meet, and which emphasises the need for co-ordinated policies and for schools to reorganise.

## Resourcing issues

Countries differ considerably in the way that special needs education is funded, and hence in the way that resources are given to schools to promote greater inclusion (Lunt and Evans, 1994; Lipsky and Gartner, 1996; Meijer, 2000). Meijer (2000) hypothesises that the types of provision that have been developed and implemented in different countries are mainly determined by funding. Provision for special educational needs (however allocated) demands an increasing proportion of countries' education budgets. In their study which looked at costs and outcomes for pupils with moderate learning difficulties in special and mainstream schools, Crowther *et al.* (1998) raised three questions:

1  Is expenditure managed efficiently so that the highest quality provision is secured at the lowest cost?
2  Is it managed equitably so that, in particular, it is deployed towards those pupils with the greatest needs?
3  Is its use effective so that pupils' needs are met and as high a level of educational outcomes as possible is produced?

On the basis of his study of different funding models of 17 European countries, Meijer (2000) suggested that 'inclusion can be achieved more easily in a decentralised model', that monitoring, inspection and evaluation procedures must be integral elements of the funding system, and finally that delegation of funds to municipalities or school 'clusters' may be an attractive option. This finding was supported by a study of LEAs in England which suggested that a more effective way of reducing requests for statements of SEN is for LEAs to delegate more funds to schools for managing SEN issues (Ainscow *et al.*, 1999).

    Formal assessment and identification (through the use of statements of special educational need in the UK, for example) may reflect the desire to protect the interests of vulnerable children by ensuring that their needs are recognised, but they also reinforce individualistic models of disability, and may lead to 'perverse incentives' as schools maximise the numbers of pupils individually identified (Lunt and Evans, 1994; Moore 2000). Croll and Moses (2000b) conclude that:

- Any attempt to use resource allocation as a means of promoting inclusion must address the question of the future of special schools which are highly costly;
- A resource allocation procedure which depends on the identification of individual children will inevitably lead to complex and bureaucratic assessment procedures (and may provide 'perverse incentives');
- The link between inclusive schools and effective schools is not clear (see Lunt and Norwich, 1999);
- The increasing expansion of the concept of SEN to include about one in four pupils in mainstream schools is not helpful, and the proportion of children for whom an individualised model of resourcing is appropriate is very low.

Following the Warnock Report (DES, 1978), which claimed that up to 20 per cent of pupils could experience learning difficulties at some time, the number of pupils identified with SEN has grown, and will continue to grow as long as resources are allocated according to individual pupils. The challenge continues to be how to provide resources to schools to meet pupils' needs in a way which is equitable and fair, and which recognises that some schools have greater numbers of pupils with SEN without leading to the identification of greater numbers of pupils. Both Moore (1999) and Gray and Dessent (1993) have provided models of LEA funding in England which aim to resource schools for greater inclusion, and provide incentives for schools to include pupils designated as having SEN.

The way that schools are resourced in respect of pupils who have learning disabilities or special educational needs crucially affects their ability to be inclusive. The maintenance of a separate special school system prevents funds being allocated to support in mainstream schools, and the growing number of pupils identified and resourced individually undermines attempts to develop more inclusive schools. Models of resourcing that target schools, and reward them for being inclusive rather than provide 'perverse incentives' for schools to identify as many individual pupils as possible, will promote inclusion.

## Evaluation of outcomes of inclusion

It is widely acknowledged that it is difficult to evaluate the outcomes of inclusive education (Madden and Slavin, 1983; Danby and Cullen, 1988; Hornby, 1992; Hegarty, 1993; Jenkinson, 1997; Feiler and Gibson, 1999; Farrell, 2000), and that the evidence on outcomes of mainstream education is largely inconclusive. In a wide-ranging international review of studies of integration for the OECD, Hegarty drew conclusions which are 'tentative at best and generally inconclusive' when evaluating the efficacy of integration in terms of a range of educational outcomes (1993: 197). A number of further studies have also failed to find conclusive evidence for the benefits of inclusive education (Farrell, 1997; Salend and Duhaney, 1999; Manset and Semmel, 1997; Hunt and Goetz, 1997). The absence of evidence for the superior performance of pupils in segregated settings has provided justification in itself for the rights of pupils to be educated in mainstream (e.g. Gartner and Lipsky, 1987). Thus as Florian points out:

> The absence of differences in educational achievement for pupils with SEN who are placed in inclusive classrooms when compared with the achievement of those in separate provision is considered supportive of inclusive education because impetus for the movement is grounded in human rights.
>
> (Florian, 1998: 107)

Although 'full inclusionists' would question the value of research into evaluation of inclusive education (e.g. Booth, 1996), 'realistic inclusionists' demand evidence that pupils' needs are being met. There are methodological difficulties with evaluation. Pupils can have a wide range of 'problems', and the segregated and inclusive settings that may be provided vary enormously. Nevertheless there are a number of meta-analyses such as those of Carlberg and Kavale (1980) and Wang and Baker (1985–6) which demonstrate overall gains in integrated as compared to segregated settings, and give cautious justification for inclusive settings. Furthermore the methodological difficulties of evaluating outcomes have led some to approach this question from a different angle by asking 'what works in inclusive education' (Sebba and Sachdev, 1997), and communicating effective practice.

Surveys that have attempted to find out parents' views about inclusion have been largely inconclusive (e.g. McDonnell, 1987; Jenkinson, 1997; and see Allen, 1999) and have not demonstrated clear support either for or against inclusion. A small number of surveys have attempted to find out the views of pupils themselves with generally inconclusive results. A number of surveys have aimed to discover the views of teachers (Giangreco *et al.*, 1993; Scruggs and Mastropieri, 1996; Vaughn *et al.*, 1996). In a meta-analysis of 28 studies on teacher perceptions of inclusion, Scruggs and Mastropieri (1996) showed that while two-thirds supported the concept of mainstreaming/inclusion, a smaller majority were willing to put this into practice. While over half felt that inclusion could provide some benefits, one-third believed that they had insufficient time, skills, training or resources. However, a number of studies have found that teachers report a change in their attitudes after the experience of including pupils designated as having disabilities in their class, and after experiencing some of the benefits both to pupils identified as being disabled and non-disabled (e.g. Giangreco *et al.*, 1993).

Although evaluation of outcomes of different provision is extremely difficult, and the results of studies are inconclusive, the absence of strong evidence for the superiority of segregated schooling gives encouragement to policies which include a wider diversity of disabilities in mainstream schools. Nevertheless, monitoring the effectiveness of provision, including its cost-effectiveness and 'value-added' effectiveness, is important for evaluating the process of inclusive schooling, and providing evidence to underpin policy commitments and initiatives.

## Strategies

A wide range of strategies that promote successful inclusion of pupils with special educational needs has been identified. These include strategies at local authority level, group of schools or 'cluster' level, and at school level.

Newham Education Authority in England makes full inclusion explicit in its Mission Statement: 'the ultimate goal of Newham's Inclusive Education policy is to make it possible for every child, whatever special educational needs they have, to attend their neighbourhood school' (Jordan and Goodey, 1996: 1) and has systematically accompanied inclusive schooling with closure of special schools. Ainscow *et al.* (1999) have described six themes which seem to be crucial to the development of more inclusive practices within LEAs:

1  policy development;
2  funding strategies;
3  processes and structures;
4  the management of change;
5  partnerships;
6  external influences.

This suggests that LEAs have a crucial role, and that policies for inclusion at LEA level need to be followed through with resourcing mechanisms which reward schools for including rather than excluding pupils, and that schools need to be supported to change their orientation and practices, and to collaborate with other schools and other agencies in order to become more inclusive.

Inter-school collaboration using 'clusters' of schools which work together, sharing resources, staff or facilities in order to enable them to meet a wider range of needs, has been set up both in the Netherlands and England and has enabled schools to support each other and to achieve some economies of scale (e.g. Dyson and Gains, 1993; Lunt *et al.*, 1994; Evans *et al.*, 1999; Hofman, 1999). Wrap-around services in the US which bring different services together to provide an integrated plan have enabled schools to support pupils with complex needs (Eber *et al.*, 1997). At the level of the school in the US, 'Adaptive Education' and the 'Adaptive Learning Environments Model' (ALEM) have attempted to address the needs of individual pupils in mainstream schools (Gartner and Lipsky, 1987), while Booth and colleagues have described ways in which individual schools have responded to the diversity of students (Booth *et al.*, 1997).

Strategies which promote inclusion of pupils with special educational needs include local authority policies, inter-school collaboration through 'clusters', inter-service collaboration such as wrap-around services, or individual school policies. The emphasis must be on enabling schools to respond to the diversity of pupils rather than on the individual placement of pupils with disabilities in mainstream schools; this involves a radical reform of schooling and 'systemic change and a national policy' (Mittler, 2000).

## Features of inclusive schools

A number of commentators in England have attempted to identify features of 'inclusive schools' (e.g. Hopkins *et al.*, 1996; Rouse and Florian, 1996; Sebba and Sachdev, 1997). These attempts have in part been linked with the wider school effectiveness movement (see Chapter 7), and considerations of pedagogy for all children (Lewis and Norwich, 2000).

Drawing on experience in England of a special school's transformation into an inclusion service, Thomas *et al.* (1998) make a number of recommendations for successful inclusive schooling. These include:

- co-ordination of services;
- staff collaboration;
- financial systems which redirect funds from segregative to inclusive provision;
- the development of an inclusive curriculum;
- positive action in the promotion of social relationships;
- commitment to neighbourhood school attendance for all children.

Further, they demonstrate the ways in which special schools may comp-
lement mainstream provision, either as resource bases, inclusive services,
or by working in close partnership with mainstream schools.

In the US, having surveyed almost 1,000 school districts, Lipsky and
Gartner (1996) identify seven key factors necessary for inclusion to be
successful:

- visionary leadership;
- collaboration;
- refocused use of assessment;
- support for staff and pupils;
- funding so that funds follow pupils;
- effective parental involvement;
- effective programme models;
- curriculum adaptation;
- adoption of effective instructional practices.

Again in the US, Giangreco (1997) identified common features of schools
where inclusive education is reported to be thriving:

- collaborative teamwork;
- developing a shared framework;
- involving families;
- general educator ownership;
- clear role relationships among professionals;
- effective use of support staff;
- determining support services;
- developing meaningful individualised education plans;
- evaluating the effectiveness of education.

Giangreco (1997) further demonstrated positive impacts of inclusive
education on pupils with and without disabilities, on professionals, and
on families. These different studies identify general features with much
in common; however, it is important to be aware that developments are
dependent to a large extent on the local context.

Vaughn and Schumm (1995), however, emphasise aspects of '*respon-*

*sible* inclusion'. On the basis of an action research project which focused on the implementation of inclusive practices in three large primary schools in large urban areas in the US, they demonstrate a more cautious and gradual approach to inclusion. They suggest components of 'responsible inclusion', such as allowing teachers to choose whether to be involved, ensuring the provision of adequate resources, maintaining a continuum of services, developing policies 'bottom up' (i.e. involving staff and parents) rather than imposing 'top-down' models without involving schools in discussion.

Many of the general characteristics of successful inclusive schooling are similar to those for effective schools, and there are those who suggest that effective schools for all are inclusive schools (e.g. Ainscow, 1998). Although this approach may help schools to become more inclusive and to cope more successfully with pupils with general disabilities, there may still be pupils (for example those with profound and multiple disabilities or those whose behaviour is challenging) whose needs mainstream schools find almost impossible to meet, and for whom alternative provision may be an appropriate consideration, given the provision currently available within most countries. The challenge for the future is for governments to develop policies and funding which encourage and require maximum inclusion and which provide appropriate incentives to schools and authorities to achieve this; for authorities to be required to translate clear government policies into coherent practices in their organisations; for resourcing and support for the diversity of all pupils in mainstream schools; and for there to be a recognition and acknowledgement of the complexity of inclusive schooling for pupils designated as having SEN which may result in a small minority of pupils being educated other than in mainstream classrooms.

# 3 Inclusive schooling in multi-ethnic societies

*David Gillborn*

This chapter examines issues related to inclusive education in multi-ethnic societies and within globalising developments. Before examining specific issues in detail there are two general points that should be appreciated. First, 'race' and ethnicity can be hugely important aspects of people's sense of identity and their experience of different life chances. However, it should not be assumed that these issues will *always* be the most significant for all individuals or in all contexts. To assume that a person's experiences and perspectives will necessarily be defined in relation to his or her ethnicity is itself a form of stereotyping. Issues of social class, gender, sexuality, age and disability discrimination, for example, intersect with 'race' inequalities and should be examined alongside ethnic diversity (McCarthy and Crichlow, 1993; Cole, 2000).

Second, the importance of 'race' and ethnic diversity cannot be judged in relation to the proportion of a population (nationally, locally or within a particular school) that is categorised (by themselves or others) as of minority ethnic heritage. In other words, schools that are largely mono-ethnic in population are not exempt from raising awareness of racism in society. The underlying issues of social justice, and the global nature of modern population and information flows, mean that an appreciation of ethnic diversity and an awareness of anti-racism are increasingly recognised as essential components of a 'good' education, regardless of local conditions.

## Terminology

The field of 'race' and ethnic diversity is characterised by long and unresolved controversies about the very words that are used to frame debate.

This reflects the nature of the central issues and the importance of what can seem, at first sight, to be matters of mere semantics. The word 'race', for example, is often placed in inverted commas to denote its contested and socially constructed nature. Although scientific orthodoxy sought for centuries to identify separate human races (largely on the basis of physical differences and assumed cultural traits), mainstream contemporary science has exposed the fallacy of such work (Solomos and Back, 1996; Mason, 2000). The markers of 'race', and the terms used to label different groups, change from one society to another and within societies over time. The socially constructed nature of these differences, however, does not diminish their power. Although terminology and the form of debate change periodically, 'race' continues to exert considerable weight in 'common-sense' and in daily interactions. The form of words used, their meanings and consequences (intended and unintended) are part of the problem itself.

Some writers now prefer the term 'minority ethnic' rather than 'ethnic minority', because the latter seemed to infer that 'ethnicity' was somehow restricted to minorities alone (see Powney *et al.*, 1998: vii). Indeed, research has increasingly highlighted that white people's notions of their own ethnic identity (although frequently implicit and assumed) are deeply implicated in patterns of discrimination and inequality. This has been part of a wider shift in the focus of research internationally such that minorities themselves are less often the focus of inquiry (a facet of earlier 'deficit' approaches that assumed any problem must lie with the minority groups). Increasingly it is the assumptions and actions of the majority community (including white pupils, teachers and policy makers) that are examined for indications of how existing inequalities in access and attainment might reflect differences in treatment and expectation (Troyna, 1993; Banks, 1994; Hazekamp and Popple, 1997; Mac an Ghaill, 1999).

An aspect of this approach is the concern expressed about 'institutional racism' following the Stephen Lawrence Inquiry (Macpherson, 1999). The concept of 'institutional racism' has a long history and, although there have been many different definitions, a common theme in most approaches is a concern with *outcomes* rather than *intentions* (Blair *et al.*, 1999).[1] The fact that inequalities may not be intended does not mean that they are accidental: the patterning of inequalities of access and/or achievement by ethnicity frequently reflects both historical and contemporary processes that systematically act to disadvantage particular minority groups.

This review is necessarily limited by the foci of previous research and the ethnic categories that have been adopted by the authors quoted. It must be remembered, however, that the chosen terms are often contested and that some of the most common categories (such as those adopted in the 1991 British Census) offer a strange combination of colour and national markers for people (e.g. Black Caribbean, Bangladeshi), many of whom were born in the UK. It is also important that groups are not forgotten simply because they do not feature prominently in most 'race' research and policy. Gypsy/Traveller children, for example, are increasingly recognised as one of the most disadvantaged groups but their needs are frequently ignored by policy makers and researchers alike (Arshad and Almeida Diniz, 1999; Ofsted, 1999). Similarly, refugee children face particular issues that are often exacerbated by racism in the so-called 'host' society (Jones and Rutter, 1998).

## Language issues

Internationally a concern with language education has been one of the most prominent issues as education systems come to terms with ethnic diversity. Teaching minority pupils the majority language is often the first (and at times the only) visible change that occurs in the education system. In England, for example, early policy approaches were built on the notion that language presented the major obstacle to achievement and that once minority pupils had learnt English there would be no need to separately address ethnic diversity at all (see Tomlinson, 1983; Edwards, 1986; Klein, 1993; Figueroa, 1995). Such assumptions not only betrayed a racist concern to 'assimilate/integrate' that amounted to an attack on minority cultures and identities, but also revealed a completely inadequate understanding of the significance of language to community identities and dynamics (see Modood *et al.*, 1997).

At that time it was not unusual for schools to segregate bilingual learners and/or forbid them to use their community languages in school: a practice that could deepen existing divisions and sent clearly racist signals to the pupils, their monolingual peers and the various communities using the school (see Taylor with Hegarty, 1985). Language is a hugely powerful community resource and education systems internationally continue to struggle to reconcile a desire to teach the majority language (in order to enable equality of access and participation) against the danger of devaluing community languages and indeed segregating pupils from mainstream provision (Alladina, 1995; Moodley, 1995; Powney *et al.*, 1998).

The debate on bilingual education and teaching English as an Additional Language (EAL) is extremely wide-ranging and often controversial: to explore all the intricacies of existing research is beyond the scope of the present review.[2] However, certain key conclusions can be drawn with a degree of certainty. First, it is clear that bilingualism is a resource and not a problem. Often practitioners and policy makers assume that speaking English as an Additional Language is a deficit that will inevitably limit pupils' achievements. It is, of course, true that minority communities have been vocal in arguing for greater language support as an essential means of aiding economic and social inclusion (Arshad and Almeida Diniz, 1999). However, it is misleading to assume that EAL status is automatically a deficit or necessarily associated with increased risk of educational failure. For example, the recent comprehensive reviews of achievement by minority ethnic pupils in England show that Indian pupils often do as well as, or better than, their white counterparts, while Bangladeshi and Pakistani pupils tend to achieve less well (Gillborn and Gipps, 1996; Pathak, 2000). Despite these variations in achievement each of these populations has a high rate of speaking a community language other than English (Modood *et al.*, 1997).

The best current survey of community language use indicates a changing and complex situation. The majority of South Asian adults are fluent in at least one language other than English, but there is a decline in the use of community languages by parents and other elders when speaking with younger family members: 'In fact about a third of Indians, African

Asians and Pakistanis normally spoke to younger family members in English. ... The Bangladeshis were the only South Asian group not yet to have experienced a linguistic decline' (Modood *et al.*, 1997: 310–11). The pattern of community language use, therefore, is varied and dynamic. The situation is complex and it is clear that there is no simple association between EAL and school performance. Although Indian pupils in England do rather better on average than their Pakistani and Bangladeshi peers, community languages are widely spoken in each group. There has been a decline in the use of community languages with young people of Indian origin but the same is also true of Pakistani households.

Additionally, there is evidence that once reasonably fluent in English, minority pupils can achieve average attainments that are higher than those of their monolingual peers. In the London Borough of Tower Hamlets, for example, there is a clear and direct association between Bangladeshi pupils' level of fluency and their attainment in examinations at age 16. As Figure 3.1 illustrates, on average bilingual pupils were attaining better results than their monolingual peers even at 'stage 3' (which is not fully fluent) and despite the fact that a greater proportion of the bilingual pupils live in poverty. These data strongly support the case for structured support to develop English language fluency as a means of raising minority attainments. However, such support seems most effective (in terms of generating high attainments) where it does not involve long-term removal from the mainstream or separation into different (lower status) teaching groups. Research from the UK and USA indicates that where EAL pupils are placed long term in different teaching groups (in low streams, tracks, bands or sets) this can limit their access to the curriculum, have a demotivating effect, and result in lower attainments (Troyna and Siraj-Blatchford, 1993; Hallam and Toutounji, 1996; Slavin, 1996; Hatcher, 1997; Green, 1999).

Bilingualism is a potentially rich resource for pupils and their schools. Contrary to the widespread assumption (among majority teachers and policy makers) that EAL represents a deficit, there is a strong case for an inclusive approach that values linguistic diversity; supports the development of English fluency; and guards against the institutionalisation of inequalities through long-term segregation on the basis of EAL status.

**Figure 3.1** *Educational attainment by stage of English and fluency*

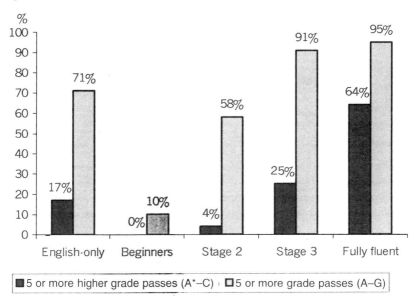

## The curriculum

As education systems move beyond the initial stages of attempting to 'assimilate' minority communities, with an overwhelming (sometimes exclusive) emphasis on language issues, the next topic for discussion is frequently the curriculum (see Mullard, 1982; Tomlinson, 1990; Melnick, 2000). In multi-ethnic areas of England and Wales, for example, early attempts were often characterised by a well-intentioned, but usually racist, portrayal of minority communities as strange and exotic. Sometimes referred to as the 'Three S's approach' – Saris, Samosas and Steel bands – the idea that promoting an understanding of lifestyles would enhance life chances is 'seductive, enduring and non-threatening' (Troyna and Carrington, 1990: 20). Moves to portray 'positive images' have also been subject to criticism that they strike a patronising tone and by highlighting a few 'exceptional cases' can be interpreted as suggesting that success is a matter of individual characteristics. Consequently, failure is again recast as a personal issue unrelated to wider structural factors and societal racism (see Banks, 1997). It is an awareness of these weaknesses that led one anti-racist critic to describe multicultural education as 'the Trojan horse of institutional racism' (Brandt, 1986: 117). In contrast, Brandt and others have argued for a distinctly anti-racist approach to curriculum reform and pedagogy that highlights the lived experiences of various minority communities and identifies racism as a long-established but changing aspect of society (Carrim, 1996).

Contemporary understandings of the role of the curriculum highlight several key findings:

- 'Permeation' does not work: where teachers, schools and indeed entire education systems have pursued a policy of 'permeation' (which claims to have multicultural content permeate the whole curriculum), the facts indicate that little meaningful change occurs. Many individual teachers, schools and whole curricular areas have remained unaltered behind a facade of supposed permeation.
- Multicultural and anti-racist content can be central to a good education across the whole curriculum: although 'permeation' often fails, so too does an additive approach that simply 'bolts-on' a token multicultural content as an afterthought or optional element. There is now a growing body of international work that addresses ways in which a multicultural and anti-racist element can become a central and valuable component in mainstream teaching across the entire curriculum and for all age groups (see, for example, Richardson and Wood, 1999).
- Anti-oppressive education is always unfinished: by its nature anti-oppressive education, including anti-racist work, must always be alive to changing forms of identities and exclusions. Racism and other forms of exclusion are far from static; even the most reflexive and dedicated schools can find themselves having to react to unexpected events and new tensions as a result of changing relations locally (say in a neighbourhood or estate), nationally and even globally (e.g. the rising anti-Islamic racism that followed the Gulf War in the early 1990s: cf. Runnymede Trust, 1997).

## School structures and teachers' expectations

The 1980s and 1990s saw a shift away from studies focusing on minority communities and pupils in isolation and towards a greater focus on the role of institutions, especially schools. This change reflected a growing recognition that earlier studies, by neglecting the role of the school and the (predominantly white) teaching force, had supported the status quo and added to the deficit discourse that positioned minorities themselves as 'the problem' (see: Troyna, 1993; Blair, 1998; Gillborn, 1998a). In particular, researchers have increasingly used qualitative approaches (especially drawing on observational and interview data) to examine how the taken-for-granted assumptions of everyday school life might actively play a role in the racialisation of success and failure in mainstream schools. In this section we briefly examine some of the key findings that relate to the role of the school.

### *Teachers' attitudes towards pupils*

Teachers' expectations for their pupils are now widely understood to have a major impact on school experience and attainment. Research has established that pupils can face markedly different expectations on the basis of their perceived ethnicity. Young people of African and Caribbean ethnic heritage, for example, are often assumed to come from unstable families that are unsupportive of education. In fact, the exact opposite appears true insofar as African Caribbean young people report greater degrees of parental support and appear more highly motivated on average than their white peers of similar social class background (Drew, 1995; Gillborn and Gipps, 1996). In the classroom, however, teachers' beliefs about particular groups can lead to them being treated very differently.

A growing number of studies argue that teachers operate with a heightened fear of disruption, and even aggression, from African Caribbean young people (Wright, 1986, 1992; Mac an Ghaill, 1988, 1994; Gillborn, 1990; Figueroa, 1991; Connolly, 1998). The situation is especially pronounced for Black young men and results in a disproportionate number of negative and critical interactions with teachers (Mirza, 1992; Sewell,

1997, 1998).[3] At one level the result of these processes can be detected in the disproportionate numbers of Black boys who are permanently excluded (this is a long-established problem in England, for example, see Majors *et al.*, 1998; SEU, 1998; Wright *et al.*, 2000).

Less obvious, but potentially damaging to a greater number of pupils, these same processes can result in Black children being placed in low status teaching groups that restrict their access to the curriculum and institutionalise inequality. In situations where teachers are invited to separate pupils into different groups on the basis of their perceived behaviour and/or 'ability', the overwhelming evidence of research is that Black pupils (especially boys) are significantly over-represented in low status groups (see: Wright, 1986; Oakes, 1990; Hallam and Toutounji, 1996; Hatcher, 1997; Gillborn and Youdell, 2000). There is no evidence that selection into separate hierarchically ordered teaching groups brings about any net improvement in attainment (gains at the top end are offset by losses elsewhere) but there is clear evidence that such practices institutionalise inequality of opportunity and attainment.

Evidence concerning teachers' treatment of South Asian students is, in some ways, less straightforward.[4] In some multi-ethnic contexts, where there are significant numbers of Black *and* South Asian students, it has been argued that the latter might be viewed more favourably, as quiet and studious. Alternatively, where South Asian students are the main or only minority group, there is evidence of more negative stereotypes coming to bear (see Mac an Ghaill, 1989; Gillborn, 1998b). Consequently, an assumption that South Asian students' home backgrounds are stable and traditional might in some circumstances be viewed as supporting high achievement and motivation, while on other occasions the same background assumptions might link to stereotypes of an oppressive home that dominates and over-aspires (see Figure 3.2).

It is impossible to predict the precise ways in which multiple beliefs and stereotypes come into play in any one context. There is a great deal of evidence, however, that the beliefs and attitudes of white teachers and pupils can have marked negative effects for South Asian pupils. I have already noted, for example, that inappropriate beliefs about language abilities might

**Figure 3.2** *The construction of stereotypes in different contexts*

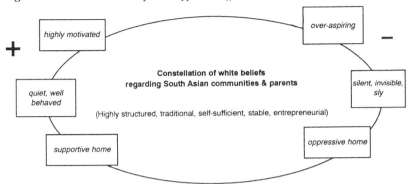

lead to some South Asian students being placed in inappropriate teaching groups and denied equal access to the curriculum and qualifications. Their lower achievements might be deemed unproblematic where teachers' expectations have been systematically lowered because of inaccurate beliefs about the potential of bilingual pupils. Compare, for example, the above data showing the greater attainments of bilingual pupils in Tower Hamlets against the view of a teacher elsewhere who described an 11-year-old pupil in the lowest teaching group as doing well 'for an ESL [English as a Second Language] pupil' (quoted in Powney *et al.*, 1998: 33).[5]

*Invisibility*

Research has also indicated that a kind of invisibility can characterise Asian pupils' experience of school. In some work this invisibility has referred to teachers' readiness to seek input from, and to praise the work of, majority students rather than their Asian peers; an issue of exclusion that can be especially pronounced for South Asian girls (Brah and Minhas, 1985; Connolly, 1998; Bhatti, 1999). On other occasions this exclusion can take a more overt form, with teachers assuming (on the basis of stereotypes such as those mentioned already) that Asian pupils (again, most often girls) will not be permitted the same freedoms as their white peers: Cecile Wright, for example, recorded the following example in her research in English primary and middle schools:

The teacher was distributing letters to the class to take home to their parents to elicit their permission [for a weekend trip]. The teacher commented to the Asian girls in the class: 'I suppose we'll have problems with you girls. Is it worth me giving you a letter, because your parents don't allow you to be away from home overnight?'

(Wright, 1992: 18)

Qualitative research has highlighted that Asian students are anything but invisible to their white peers; Asian boys and girls are frequently recipients of racist harassment, often verbal but sometimes physical. From written evidence submitted to the Swann Report (Swann, 1985) through to recently published school- and interview-based studies, a clear pattern emerges in relation to this racist victimisation (Gillborn and Gipps, 1996; Connolly, 1998; Bhatti, 1999):

- Teachers frequently ignore the victimisation or take disproportionate action against Asian students when they defend themselves;
- Asian pupils (and their white peers) view teachers' failure to act against racist victimisation as a sign of the low priority accorded such matters in the real life of schools beyond the rhetorical commitment to equal opportunities seen in so many presentations to the outside world.

### *Ignoring racism*
Bhatti (1999) reports the following as 'typical' of the examples she was offered by Asian young children and adults when discussing problems that they had encountered with teachers:

One day after the test Mrs Hinds was calling out names of kids who got high marks. Someone asked who got the lowest marks and the teacher said 'Zafar Ali'. Someone shouted at the back 'All Pakis are dumb'. Everyone laughed. *Everyone* heard it, even Mrs Hinds.... She didn't do nothing. She pretended she never heard it. There was no punishment, no nothing. She pretended she never heard it. There was no punishment, no.... Then the same damn teachers tell you to ignore it, just like *they* do.

(Bhatti, 1999: 188, original emphasis)

A further example, from the same study, illustrates how a failure to engage with racism can lead to a spiralling of conflict and resentment. Simply ignoring racism not only fails to counter it, but can encourage further racism and even violence. The situation started with pupil racism in the classroom and a teacher's reaction. As the description begins, Shakeel and John have been arguing, with John stating that 'Pakis' cheat:

> The atmosphere was getting charged. Miss Paine was busy writing the date on the blackboard. Lot of general noise in class which sounds incoherent on tape. Shakeel looking very provoked, shoved the book aside and pushed the chair back. Lull in noise level.
>
> *John:* Look at him! Paki Pakora [latter said in a near whisper but audible to Shakeel, Asad and me].
>
> *Shakeel:* I'll smash your face in, you clown [said very loudly].
>
> *AP:* [Turning around] Right that's enough. Shakeel leave the class this minute.
>
> *Shakeel:* But Miss...
>
> *AP:* Out! Go and stand outside ... God these boys!

The observer goes on to explain that 'Other children had also been making a noise and not just Shakeel. It had seemed surprising to me at the time that Miss Paine did not keep the quarrelling parties behind to try and ascertain the circumstances which had led to the incident' (Bhatti, 1999: 192). The next day both John and Shakeel were involved in a fight between three white boys and three Asian peers, 'Miss Paine's decision to send an Asian boy out instead of punishing both boys was racist in its outcome if not in intention. Had both boys been Asian or white the matter might not have had racist connotations' (Bhatti, 1999: 192).

The example shows how a racialised conflict between pupils can escalate when teachers fail to act against racism: Bhatti's analysis does not call for any special treatment for the Asian pupil, rather she identifies the need for a sound approach to disciplinary issues, especially between pupils of different ethnicities. Had the teacher taken the time to explore the conflict, she would have had an opportunity to act against pupil racism; as it was, the victim of racist harassment was disciplined and the conditions created for a violent escalation of the conflict. Research illustrates, therefore, several ways in which failure to engage with ethnic diversity and racism (in the curriculum, in selection structures, and in the behaviour of teachers and pupils) can have the effect of excluding minority pupils from the opportunities and attainments available to other students.

### Communication with parents

Parents of minority ethnic heritage can also find themselves excluded from the opportunities available to others. In Chapter 5, a range of issues related to parental involvement are discussed; at this point it is necessary to highlight additional barriers that can hinder the inclusion of minority ethnic parents. Once again, language issues are usually among the first to be considered.

Producing written material in a range of community languages is a basic first step towards the inclusion of some minority ethnic communities. This can extend from guidance leaflets and information produced nationally, through to individual school prospectuses and newsletters. In some ethnically diverse areas, schools and other organisations point to the sheer number of languages that are spoken as an argument against producing materials in community languages. However, in many cases simply focusing on the two or three most common languages will greatly improve the possibilities for community involvement.

Written materials are only the start. Meaningful involvement cannot take place where teachers and parents cannot communicate directly, and the use of pupils as translators creates considerable difficulties. In these situations schools require additional resources to employ bilingual assistants who can help at parents' evenings and other such events. Indeed, having a full-time contact person in the school, fluent in the community language(s) locally, can be an enormously helpful addition.

Beyond these relatively obvious points there are a great many other things that can encourage genuine participation. Building relations with local community groups can be a useful start, but throughout these processes the mainstream organisations must interrogate their own actions for unintended bias or other problems. For example, if attendance at parental meetings is low, is the information getting home? Is the nature of the partnership with parents understood? Are there problems of transport, working hours or fear of harassment in the street? Any or all of these issues could be a factor and there is much that schools and local authorities can do to overcome them.

## Policy and practice

I have already commented on the diverse and changing range of words and concepts used to describe and explore ethnic diversity. Over recent decades a variety of terms have been used to describe an approach to education that seeks to engage with ethnic diversity and bring about greater 'race' equality. In Britain during the 1980s, in particular, there was a heated dispute between those favouring 'multicultural' education and those proposing an 'anti-racist' approach (see, for example, Jeffcoate, 1984; Mullard, 1984; Brandt,1986; Lynch, 1986). Put crudely, the former stressed the need for curricular change while the latter adopted a more thorough critique of racism as a structural concern that had to be opposed throughout the education system (see above on the curriculum).

In the USA, the term multiculturalism has been used more broadly to include a variety of approaches, some of which more closely approximate the British model of anti-racism. In contrast, many European writers presently use the term 'intercultural' to relate to a similar field of theory and practice. In order to move beyond the internal disputes of the 1980s, others have attempted to combine different approaches under a single heading, or suggest new ways in which practitioners, policy makers and researchers can learn from the mistakes of the past by assuming a more self-critical and flexible stance. In particular, the notions of critical multiculturalism and critical anti-racism are gaining prominence in current debates in parts of the UK, USA and Africa (McLaren, 1995; Kinchloe and Steinberg, 1997; Carrim and Soudien, 1999; May, 1999; Gillborn, 2000).

Out of this changing and uncertain array of different terms, concepts and strategies, some central elements are emerging. At the school level there is a growing body of work that identifies practical and proven ways forward. Beyond this, however, it is vital that education policy and practice is situated within a recognition of the powerful ways in which 'race' inequalities can work through and be reinforced by policy.

There is clear evidence that 'colour-blind' policies have not reduced inequality; in some circumstances they encourage greater inequalities of opportunity. In England, for example, the successive education reforms of the late 1980s and 1990s made virtually no mention of ethnic diversity and included no meaningful safeguards against racism. Consequently the period witnessed growing gaps in attainment between Black and white pupils and an increasing over-representation of Black pupils among permanent exclusions/expulsions from school (Majors *et al.*, 1998; Demack *et al.*, 2000; Gillborn and Youdell, 2000; Wright *et al.*, 2000). In a situation where so many factors are structured by existing 'racial' inequality (such as income, place of residence, level of parental education), to behave as if 'race' were not a significant factor can leave the way clear for present inequalities to be compounded.

Additionally, 'colour-blind' approaches have traditionally been associated with a situation where 'race' inequalities are deemed an inappropriate area for policy intervention or even viewed as a result of weaknesses or deficits in the people themselves. In these circumstances, 'colour-blindness' does not amount to promoting a 'level playing field' (as is usually supposed) but in fact operates as a form of 'race' denial, effectively ruling out any critical examination of the extent of 'racial' inequalities and how they might be countered (see Apple, 1999).

Relatedly, several writers have noted the danger that talk of 'inclusion' can sometimes operate in a very general way as a blanket term, deflecting attention from 'race' inequalities. The notion of 'equal opportunities', for example, is often used broadly, but ultimately interpreted as simply meaning gender inequalities (Arshad and Almeida Diniz, 1999). One facet of this has been a reluctance among some policy makers, researchers and practitioners to specifically address ethnic diversity. In this way inequalities can go unnoticed and unattended (Gillborn and Gipps, 1996).

In order to examine current patterns of experience and attainment, it is necessary to establish rigorous and sensitive systems of ethnic monitoring. There is widespread agreement that monitoring is a first step towards greater 'race' equality. Credible moves to improve 'race' equality and inclusion cannot be sustained in the absence of basic information concerning, for example, the make up of the school population; the different courses that pupils follow; their rates of achievement at different points in education; and the kinds of destination they attain. In isolation, of course, ethnic monitoring does not diagnose the precise nature of any problem, nor does it prescribe a solution: monitoring is a necessary part of educational inclusion strategies in a multi-ethnic society, but it is not sufficient alone.

Finally, it should be noted that despite the wealth of research in this field internationally, there is no simple blueprint for raising the attainment of minority pupils, countering racism and achieving inclusion in multi-ethnic schools. Prior experience has pointed to numerous ways forward, but it is clear that such moves are always conditional: as we have noted, even schools with a long history of successful work in this field can find themselves wrong-footed by events locally, nationally or even globally (Gillborn, 1995).

## Strategies for inclusive education in a multi-ethnic society

Notwithstanding the complexities noted above, the research in this area has identified several components that help establish and sustain greater inclusion and 'race' equality in education:

- *Strong leadership on equal opportunities and inclusion is essential*
  From the national level, to the local authority, and to the individual school principal; it is essential that equal opportunities and inclusion are signalled as genuine concerns that are taken seriously. In the absence of such high profile support, inclusion policies lapse into rhetoric and become token.

- *Developing and communicating high expectations of all pupils linked to a clear undertaking that underachievement by any group is unacceptable*
  This is especially important in challenging the powerful stereotypes of lower achievement that are often associated with certain minority groups and which can become self-fulfilling prophecies when institutionalised via different treatment and lower expectations in the school, for example through separation into lower teaching groups.
- *Ethnic monitoring*
  Developing useful and widely understood forms of ethnic monitoring is now viewed an essential first step in working towards inclusion and equitable treatment. While monitoring alone is not sufficient, it is a necessary part of the wider institutional systems and mechanisms that deliver equal opportunities. Such systems should be developed sensitively and with regard to community concerns; however, data must be generated across all institutions, in comparable forms, and be open to rigorous scrutiny. From the national level to the individual school, ethnic monitoring can provide essential information about current inequalities of opportunity and achievement: this information can be a powerful spur to action.
- *Seeking and using parental and pupil perspectives*
  Pupils have an especially keen sense of social justice. There are simple and effective ways of seeking the views of pupils and parents. These can be a source of immediate benefit and, when taken seriously, help build further links of mutual trust and respect.
- *An open and inclusive whole school ethos*
  Schools should work to develop an inclusive school ethos where pupils are encouraged to share their concerns within an atmosphere that is supportive.
- *Designing and enacting clear whole school policies on racist harassment*
  As part of schools' work against all forms of harassment there should be an explicit recognition of racist harassment and agreed procedures for recording and acting on each incident.

None of these aspects, in isolation, guarantees success but together they appear to be central elements in creating a strong inclusive education.[6]

## Notes

1 The Stephen Lawerence Inquiry defined institutional racism as: 'The collective failure of an organisation to provide an appropriate and professional service to people because of their colour, culture, or ethnic origin. It can be seen or detected in processes, attitudes and behaviour which amount to discrimination through unwitting prejudice, ignorance, thoughtlessness and racist stereotyping which disadvantage minority ethnic people' (Macpherson, 1999: 28).

2 There is no universally accepted way of describing teaching for minority students that addresses their use of the majority tongue. In line with most current writing in the field in the UK, I adopt the term English as an Additional Language (EAL) which is often used in preference to earlier terms such as 'English as a Second Language' (ESL/E2L). Elsewhere researchers prefer to refer to bilingual, multilingual or Limited English Proficient (LEP) students (see Minami and Ovando, 1997).

3 The term 'Black' is here used to refer to people with family origins in Africa and/or the Caribbean, and reflects the most common form of self-identification among that group. Although the term is sometimes used to refer to all minority groups who experience white racism, such use is generally decreasing in recognition of the multiple forms of racism and the fact that many people so labelled reject the more general use of the term (see Modood *et al.,* 1994).

4 The majority of research on 'Asian' pupils' experiences has focused on those with family origins in India, Pakistan and Bangladesh. There is a small but important literature on other Asian children's schooling, including those of Chinese ethnic origin. In view of the limits of space on the current review, however, I will focus in the main on the literature pertaining to South Asian pupils.

5. The pupil in question was of Japanese ethnic heritage but had been educated in Scotland for seven years.

6 For further details see: ALAOME, 2000; Amin *et al.,* 1997; Blair and Bourne, 1998; Dadzie, 2000; Green, 1999; Gillborn, 1995; Gillborn and Gipps, 1996; Oakes and Lipton, 1999; Ofsted, 1999; Osler, 1997; Richardson and Wood, 1999; Siraj-Blatchford, 1994; Weekes and Wright, 1999.

# 4 Gender equity and reform for inclusive schooling

*Simon Warren*

The shifting conceptualisations of inclusive schooling and equity, as described in Chapter 1, have had a significant impact on gender issues in schools. For example, the past twenty years have witnessed two parallel and interconnected developments in education in England: the year-on-year improvement in overall academic achievement and the 'closing' of the gender 'gap' (Ofsted and EOC, 1996; Arnot *et al.*, 1999). Since the late 1990s there has been a dramatic shift away from a focus on equal opportunities for girls, to a concern with the apparent underachievement of boys. In order to conduct a robust analysis of attempts to address this concern and analyse its importance for inclusive schooling, it is first essential that the 'problem' be clearly defined.

## Gender and achievement in perspective

In England and Wales, official statistics based on an analysis of SATs, GCSE results, Ofsted inspections, and reviews of achievement (Ofsted and EOC, 1996) have demonstrated a sizeable increase in girls' educational attainment across all sectors; some entry into traditionally male subjects; continuation rates in post-compulsory education; and entry into university. This improvement in girls' educational performance has been partly attributed to their continuing advantage (compared to boys) in English, and their improvements in mathematics and science. This has occurred in a context where overall achievement has been rising, but where boys' performance has not risen at the same rate or to the same level. Even more significant is the assertion that we are witnessing an inversion of the gender gap in favour of girls (Arnot *et al.*, 1999). Changes in patterns of achievement in terms of gender, however, are somewhat offset by the widening gap between groups on the basis of social class and 'racial' differences (Demack *et al.*, 2000; Gillborn and Mirza, 2000; see also Chapter 3).

Furthermore, girls continue to be channelled towards traditionally 'female' subjects and are less likely to be placed in the higher examination tier for subjects such as mathematics (Gillborn and Youdell, 2000; Stobart *et al.*, 1992). Girls continue to demonstrate a preference for English and humanities, while boys tend to prefer science, mathematics, information technology and physical education. These patterns are reflected in A-level and post-16 choice (Ofsted and EOC, 1996; Arnot *et al.*, 1998). Also, higher general attainment by girls does not automatically translate into equality in the market-place; subject choice in university; or post-higher education destination (Arnot *et al.*, 1996; Powney, 1996; Riddell, 1999; Power *et al.*, 1999).

While girls' overall performance has improved, it is clearly not the case that all girls achieve equally. Similarly, not all boys underachieve. Indeed, significant numbers of boys continue to perform well above average, even in traditionally 'female' subjects such as English and foreign languages (see Murphy and Elwood, 1998). The picture is much more complex than is allowed for in most popular discussions of the 'problem'. A more detailed analysis of available figures suggests that there is far more overlap between the attainment of boys and girls; differential relative attainment in particular subjects; and different patterning at different levels (see Fielding *et al.*, 1999).

Contemporary studies also direct attention to the connection between successful academic achievement and the social construction of middle-class male identities. Of particular interest is the cultivation of 'effortless' achievement, where boys are keenly aware of their academic positions, but also conscious that they threaten their high status masculinity by being too public about their efforts (Aggleton, 1987; Heward, 1988; Mac an Ghaill, 1994; Warren, 1997; Power *et al.*, 1998). On the other hand, disengagement from official school culture, active resistance and the dismissal of school work as the occupation of 'sissies' and 'wimps' has been described as key characteristics of some traditional male working-class responses to school. More recently, it has been argued that resistance to school continues to be an element in shaping working-class male identities (Connell, 1996a; Mac an Ghaill, 1994).

The relationship between ethnicity and boys' underachievement is complex (see also Chapter 3). A new analysis of previously unpublished data indicates that Indian, Pakistani, Bangladeshi and African Caribbean girls tend to do better than their male peers (Gillborn and Mirza, 2000). Of pressing concern is the way that certain groups (especially African Caribbean and Bangladeshi young men) may increasingly find themselves pushed toward a 'macho', anti-school position. Qualitative research has begun to highlight ways in which youth subcultures, media representations and teacher expectations come to construct the form of hypersexualised and anti-authoritarian masculinity that is at odds with academic attainment (Back, 1996; Debnath, 1998; Sewell, 1998).

## Triggers for change in gender equity

Why has the public focus on equity issues in education become overwhelmingly dominated by a concern with the apparent underachievement of boys? And how might this effect the character of gender reform as part of an inclusive schools programme? By dominating the gender equity debate this policy and public focus on boys' underachievement can give the impression that the previous concern with girls' underachievement is no longer relevant. Similarly, the historical concern within British education about the relationship between social class and educational advantage also appears to be marginalised. To understand how this has occurred it is important to look at the dynamic social shifts in three inter-related contexts – the macro-political, the institutional and the inter-personal.

### *The macro-political context*
Two important structural shifts in society – the economic and social – partly account for the emergence of the contemporary concern with boys' educational achievement. In the UK, during the post-war period, both the

welfare state and the national industrial policy presumed a fairly large and stable male manual workforce. Post-war industrial and economic growth also saw the increasing size of a new service class, opening up new forms of social mobility. However, the social, economic and political assumptions embodied in both industrial and welfare institutions were to be increasingly questioned as the UK entered a deep structural economic crisis in the mid-1970s.

There are a number of key features that characterise the new economic landscape:

• The social and financial services sector has become increasingly important in the traditional industrialised economies;
• The labour force has become increasingly organised around a technologically skilled core and a semi- or unskilled periphery of low-paid and insecure employment (Ainley, 1993; Kumar, 1992; Lipietz, 1992);
• There has been a massive influx of women into the labour market, though most of these jobs are part-time and low paid (Jensen, 1989).
• Working practices are changing due to technological developments (Lipietz, 1992).

Changes in the economic landscape have disrupted the relative stability in male manual employment. These changes have also called for different kinds of knowledge and skills, particularly technological, communicative and group work skills (Brown and Lauder, 1992, 1996). At the same time, women's social and cultural positions are changing (see: Arnot *et al.*, 1996; ONS, 1998), and are reflected in the:

• increased participation of women in the labour market;
• increased entry of women into traditionally male-dominated fields;
• increased entry of women into higher education;
• improvement in the overall educational achievement of women;
• increase in single-person households, particularly including women.

## The institutional context – government, local education authorities and schools

There has been a shift in governmental concerns within England and Wales since the 1970s, with changing emphasis between 'equality of opportunity' and 'standards'. This shift in policy concerns has an impact on the distribution of resources and opportunities for gender reform in education.

In the 1970s and early 1980s equality of opportunity in education was characterised by a predominant concern with the systematic inequality suffered by girls (see Arnot *et al.*, 1996; Arnot *et al.*, 1999). The knowledge base for these concerns was provided by feminist research into girls' experience of the classroom (French and French, 1993; Stanley, 1993), and the gendered nature of the curriculum and school organisation (Spender, 1984; Stanworth, 1988). In part, this reflected the policy research focus on the micro-detail of inequality (Whitty, 1985) and specifically feminist concerns with elevating female experience and voices in policy debates (Stanley and Wise, 1993). On the basis of this knowledge base, feminist educators argued for the need for 'girl friendly schooling' (Whyte *et al.*, 1985). This approach suggested a number of strategies that could improve girls' educational performance and experience of schooling. These included the development of programmes for encouraging girls into traditionally male and high status subjects such as mathematics and the physical sciences; raising girls' academic and employment aspirations through the provision of positive role models; revealing the gender bias in the curriculum; and challenging the masculine character of the 'good pupil' (Walkerdine, 1988; Walkerdine and the Girls and Mathematics Unit, 1989).

The production of a knowledge base, alone, is not enough to translate empirical evidence into informed policy and practice. Wider social currents, particularly the growing impact of feminism on British society and the cultural shifts associated with this, have been identified as providing a legitimating framework for an emergent gender reform programme in education (Arnot *et al.*, 1999). In England and Wales, the passing of the Sex Discrimination Act 1977 opened up educational spaces for feminist educators to begin constructing 'girl friendly schooling'. A number of projects emerged from this aimed at encouraging girls into science and mathematics: Girls Into Science and Technology; Girls and Technology Education; and Girls Into Mathematics. Although these represented national networks, they were essentially locally-based projects of committed teachers.

In the UK, the government was increasingly concerned about the apparent lack of appropriate skills in the labour market and the need for education to furnish those skills. Government funding became available for vocationally oriented programmes. These were aimed specifically at the 14–16 age group. Feminists identified the opportunity to pursue their objectives through such programmes. Consequently, gender equity issues related to girls' attainment and labour market prospects became a characteristic of the Technical and Vocational Education Initiative (TVEI) and other vocational projects. TVEI had an explicit commitment to gender equality. This also meant that many of the most sustained gender reform programmes occurred in secondary schools (Skelton, 1989; Weiner, 1990, 1994; Frith and Mahony, 1994; Arnot *et al.*, 1996).

A growing focus on standards has drawn attention to the persistent underachievement of particular groups of students, in particular the gender differential in attainment (Ofsted and EOC, 1996). In England and Wales, Ofsted increasingly required schools to produce equal opportunities policies (Arnot *et al.*, 1996). The compulsory nature of the National Curriculum also meant that girls were not formally denied access to traditionally male subjects, at least not until GCSE subject choices towards the end of secondary schooling (Gillborn and Youdell, 2000).

Although the statistics on the gender differentials in attainment also indicated the persistence in a gender division in subject choice for GCSE, it was boys' relative underachievement in English and modern foreign languages that became the focus for official concern. Shifts in the economy and the forms of knowledge and skills perceived to be required by a knowledge economy, placed greater emphasis on communication, group work and creative thinking. These are cognitive and inter-personal modes of engagement often associated with 'femaleness'. In this context boys could be perceived to be disadvantaged in the changing labour market.

This interpretation of the shift in focus on boys' underachievement is further reinforced when it is considered that the two most significant improvements in girls' academic attainment have been in the traditionally male subjects of mathematics and science. Policy makers might then be seen to view boys as doubly disadvantaged. This interpretation is given greater weight when girls' improved academic attainment is publicly expressed in terms of boys' disadvantage, the need for strategies to improve boys' attainment in relationship to girls' and the lack of celebration for girls' and teachers' achievements. This focus (on boys' underachievement) negates girls' improved attainment and draws attention away from other sources and outcomes of disadvantage, discrimination and underachievement.

Within the UK, the election of a Labour government in 1997 signalled new shifts in education policy. Most significantly a commitment to tackling underachievement, especially in the most deprived areas, as the predominant meaning of equal opportunities. For example, in England and Wales, *Excellence in Schools* (DfEE, 1997b) outlines what the government perceives as being the most effective strategies for raising attainment in schools – target-grouping, fast-tracking, accelerated learning, systematic teaching of thinking skills, homework, extra-curricular study support, mentoring, improving attendance and home support. There have been a number of recent reviews of strategies deployed by schools and education authorities to raise achievement, including that of boys, which demonstrate that these strategies are becoming common currency (Brooks *et al.*, 1999; Ofsted, 1999; Sukhnandan, 1999; Sukhnandan *et al.*, 2000). *Excellence in Schools* argues that these are 'proven' successful strategies, despite the need for further evidence to support this claim.

There is a need to scrutinise the gendered (or racialised or social-class) assumptions in curriculum content and pedagogy (Francis, 2000). For example, strategies for raising boys' attainment may have the unintended consequence of undermining girls' improved performance. Similarly, appropriate attention might not be given to the barriers to women's entry to and movement within the labour market, and that academic achievement does not necessarily translate into economic advantage. Finally, although these strategies may indeed raise overall levels of attainment, this may occur in a context of a widening attainment gap, with African Caribbean and working-class students concentrated at the lower levels of attainment.

## The inter-personal context

Recent research suggests that the new spaces for women's social and economic improvement connects with the social constructions of school-girls as 'quiet', 'sensible', 'mature' and 'hardworking' (Francis, 2000). While these constructions of schoolgirl femininity, in the past, served to disadvantage girls, in the new contexts they appear to be benefiting them. Francis (2000) points out that feminists working in the 1970s highlighted how the male (middle-class) pupil personified the good learner (see Walkerdine, 1988). Although it is unclear to what extent boys have become cognisant with and accommodated to the social, economic and cultural shifts outlined above (see the different perspectives put forward by Arnot *et al.*, 1999, and Francis, 2000), research does suggest that boys' constructions of masculinity still largely position them negatively in relation to school and the curriculum (Wexler, 1992; Mac an Ghaill, 1994; Jackson and Salisbury, 1996; Salisbury and Jackson, 1996; Francis, 1998, 2000).

This is perhaps demonstrably so in the persistence of particular forms of heterosexuality. Dominant constructions of masculinity, in particular, seem to require boys to distance themselves from anything that is feminine and to be seen as heterosexually active and knowledgeable (especially in secondary school) (Mac an Ghaill, 1994; Connolly, 1998; Epstein and Johnson, 1998; Francis, 1998). Girls are often positioned as objects of male attraction. Consequently, boys will 'police' girls' behaviour. Similarly, boys' behaviours are 'policed'. This policing often occurs in low-level ways through the use of derisory and sexually loaded language (Kehily and Nayak, 1997; Connolly, 1998; Kenway *et al.*, 1998). However, these behaviours can take on more aggressive forms involving sexual harassment or the use of violence (Jackson and Salisbury 1996; Salisbury and Jackson, 1996; Epstein and Johnson, 1998).

Schools often find it very difficult to deal with sexual harassment. Consequently a combination of student and teacher collusion and institutional inactivity means that these behaviours can become legitimised and even institutionalised. This kind of public validation of masculine heterosexuality as the 'norm' includes the threat of being accused of being 'gay'. The contentious debate about Section 28 of the Local Government Act 1988 in England and Wales (and Clause 2A in Scotland) may then be seen as possibly legitimising harassment of lesbian and gay students, or just boys and girls who do not fit the expected norm. Recent research into the experience of lesbian and gay students highlights the endemic nature of the harassment they receive (Epstein, 1994; Douglas *et al.*, 1997; Douglas *et al.*, 2000). This research has also highlighted the confusion and fear caused by Section 28 in England and Wales. This has meant that teachers and youth workers have found it difficult to provide support to students, heterosexual as well as lesbian, gay and bisexual students. This results in exposing these students to bullying and harassment. This must be an issue of concern for any programme of inclusive schooling.

## Reflections on gender reform work

Kenway *et al.* (1998), commenting on educational gender reform work in Australia, remark that, although we know a lot about gender differentials in attainment, subject choice and labour market participation and position; that we know a lot about the micro-detail of gender construction, its complex interlacing with social class, 'race', ethnicity, disability and sexuality; the interrelationship between academic and gender identities: we know very little about the impact of gender reform work in schools. Similar concern about the general lack of evaluation of gender reform work has been raised in the UK (Frith and Mahony, 1994; Weiner, 1994). Questions have also been raised about the appropriateness of applying compensatory models of gender reform work, developed in response to girls' disadvantage, to boys (see Salisbury and Jackson, 1996).

These reflections on gender reform work highlight a number of issues pertinent to the development of inclusive schools.

*Emphasis on 'management' rather than 'curriculum' issues*

Within an emphasis on 'management', concern was mainly expressed in terms of inappropriate behaviours, for example, disruption and aggression shown by boys and lack of assertiveness by girls, rather than what was taught, how it was taught and the materials used.

*Students constructed as 'lacking'*

As well as raising expectations and widening academic and occupational horizons, the use of positive role models and anti-sexist programmes could also produce the feeling that the students themselves were the problem. Girls could feel that their 'lack' of assertiveness or desire to enter tradition-ally male subject areas was the problem. Similarly, mobilising boys' feelings of guilt, shame and anxiety around masculinity denied the possi-bility that boys could invest in change. Students could be infantilised and the emotional work involved in gender reform denied.

*Lack of explicit anti-sexist work*

The lack of any explicit anti-sexist work (with a curriculum emphasis) might shield girls from boys' behaviours but did not challenge them. The complexities of daily interactions in the classroom may not be addressed. Controversial issues, such as dealing with sexual harassment and homo-phobia, might not be dealt with if explicit anti-sexist and anti-homophobic work was not carried out.

*Issues associated with using single-sex work*

The use of single-sex groups has been recognised as providing spaces for girls to imagine different futures for themselves. It has also been suggested that single-sex teaching can improve girls' academic performance. While this cannot be dismissed, girls' continued academic improvement has occurred in the context of co-educational schools. The use of single-sex classes or teaching groups has often been used as a classroom manage-ment strategy without any attention to the gendered nature of the curriculum or sexist classroom interactions.

## Complicity in 'boys' work

Recently there have been suggestions that boys can be encouraged to take a more positive view of reading and the curriculum through the use of more 'masculine' reading material or homework clubs in football stadiums. These suggestions raise concerns about possible complicity in the very constructions of masculinity that marginalise and oppress girls and other boys. Accepting that there are different kinds of reading material 'appropriate' for girls and boys invites the spectre of there being 'appropriate' subjects for girls and boys (Francis, 2000). It also reinforces the idea that there are immutable psychological or genetic differences between girls and boys, an idea that has very little scientific support. The redistribution of resources towards 'football and literacy' or 'football and homework' schemes appears to reward the very 'laddish' behaviour that constrains many boys' academic development. It can also send out signals that legitimate the dominance of cultures of football associated with a physically assertive masculinity, ignoring those girls and boys who are not interested in football or who actually feel threatened by its masculine cultures.

## Strategies for gender and inclusive schools

Drawing on recent reviews, expositions and evaluations (Arnot *et al.*, 1996, 1998, 1999; Connell 1996a, b; Jackson and Salisbury, 1996; Kenway *et al.*,1998), it is possible to outline the goals and forms of gender work that can contribute positively to the development of inclusive schools.

### *Goals of gender work*
### *Knowledge*

This entails students and teachers engaging with a critical examination of gender: the examination of how gender identities are constructed; and how particular constructions position individuals as marginal or subordinate (and the pain that goes with that). Gender knowledge involves understanding how gender constructions can distance students from important areas of knowledge and skill, for example the need for boys to engage with English, languages and communication skills. Gender knowledge also refers to the need to be able 'to act differently in the immediate, everyday world and about how to be an advocate for change' (Kenway *et al.*, 1998). Such knowledge work could be developed through the kind of critical literacy work advocated by Davies (1989, 1993) or through the gender workshops used by Salisbury and Jackson (1996).

*Good human relationships*
This involves a range of related areas including personal, social and health education, and sex and relationships education. This goal would encompass aspects of anti-sexist and anti-homophobic work. The discussion above has illustrated how the world of the classroom is not just that of the curriculum. Academic, gender and sexual identities are constructed in relation to each other. For instance, constructions of male identities that involve an assertive heterosexuality can lead to various forms of 'policing' of girls and other boys' behaviours. This 'policing' can be extremely damaging to other students, and distract also some boys from engaging positively with the curriculum. Inclusive schooling has to incorporate more than just formal equal access to the curriculum. Such access can also only be ensured by attending to the development of good social relations among students and between students and teachers.

*Justice*
The goal of justice involves three elements: the effects of processes of gender construction, the practices of schools that produce justice or injustice, and the quality of education. The discussion of which girls and boys are underachieving highlights the need to understand that a primary focus on aggregate levels of attainment misdirects attention from the particular patterns of achievement and underachievement in schools. This can lead to viewing (all) boys as needing compensatory measures or that (all) girls are now achieving well. For instance, processes of masculine construction can 'disrupt the education of particular groups of boys, who are disadvantaged in class and ethnic terms' (Connell, 1996b: 223). Similarly, although constructions of the 'quiet schoolgirl' may be providing some

girls with productive resources, this is not equally so for all girls. The particular practices of schools, for example, setting, curriculum organisation, institutional weighting given to subject areas, can act as amplifiers for certain gender constructions. Schools need to examine how they influence, and perhaps sustain, particular forms of femininity and masculinity. Importantly, education transmits social as well as academic messages. Inclusive education should transmit notions of justice. The work of schools, including that of teacher–student relations, needs to address this issue.

*The forms of gender work*
Two forms of gender work can be defined:

• Gender-specific
These are projects or programmes aimed specifically at boys or girls as groups. These will tend to be small-scale and intimate, involving discussion and debate. Gender-specific approaches might usually deal with 'sensitive' subjects and where gender-specific environments are judged to be more productive. Questions about the gender of the teacher co-ordinating such projects needs to be considered carefully.

• Gender-relevant
These would involve both girls and boys and often entail a thematic approach. For instance, a whole school behaviour strategy could highlight the gender dimensions of different behaviours as well as trying to tackle bullying. Gender-relevant approaches might be institution oriented, for example redesigning the curriculum or timetable. In the classroom, the standpoint of the 'other' (non-dominant masculinity, lesbian and gay perspective) may be taken, challenging the 'taken-for-granted' nature of dominant forms of gender construction.

Inclusive schools need to recognise their part in amplifying particular notions of gender; and develop their role in promoting inclusive and equitable gender processes and practices.

# 5 Parental involvement and voice in inclusive schooling

*Carol Vincent*

Parental involvement in education is largely seen as a 'good thing' by the teaching profession, education policy makers and parents themselves. However, there is considerable uncertainty over the purposes of parental involvement, and what form initiatives and policies in general should take (Blair and Waddington, 1997). The rhetoric is one of 'partnership' between teacher and parent, but the actualisation of this relationship is a process fraught with contestation and confusion. It can be argued that the term 'partnership' has become a 'condensation symbol'. Briefly, this is a term assumed to engender positive emotions and feelings, but, in actuality, lack exact and agreed meaning. References to home–school 'partnership' are used routinely, to refer to a whole host of different practices, intentions and expectations.

Despite this ambiguity, a review of the literature suggests that the following understandings of parental roles can be identified:

- to raise children's achievement (parent as educator);
- to increase the degree of congruence between home and school (parent as complementor);
- to offer parents support (parent education and training);
- to offer teachers support (parents as classroom helpers and fund-raisers);
- to hold teachers accountable for their performance (parents as consumers);
- to introduce lay influence in the governance of school, introducing different perspectives and expertise, and giving 'the community' a voice in the running of local schools (parent governors and other lay governors);

- to offer parents as citizens the right to be involved in the decision-making processes within public sector institutions such as schools (parents as participants, parents as citizens).

It can be seen that not all these various interpretations are complementary; indeed most proceed from very different understandings of what the 'appropriate' role is for lay adults within schools.

A second important general point is that while the term 'parental involvement' is widely used, research has shown that in effect the parent who liaises with the school, takes part in school-organised activities, and helps with and monitors children's learning is, in the overwhelming majority of cases, the mother (David, 1993; David *et al.*, 1993; Ribbens, 1994; Reay, 1998). This phenomenon appears to hold across most social class and ethnic groups. Changing socio-economic circumstances are relevant here as there has been a notable increase in mothers returning to work (and often full-time) over the last 10–15 years (DfEE, 1998b; see also Chapter 4). This means that many mothers are simply not available to fulfil the traditional maternal role of helper in the primary classroom. Indeed, it should be noted that this increase in working mothers takes place in a general context of intensification of work for those who have it (Moss, 1999). Social trends also reveal an increase in lone-parent families, the majority of which are headed by women (ONS, 1998). Again, time and often money is limited for these mothers (Standing, 1999).

A third contextual point starts from an extremely obvious statement: that parents are highly heterogeneous, differentiated by social class, ethnicity, gender, age, religion, language and familiarity with the state education system as well as a host of more minor indicators. Schools are also, though not to such great extent, heterogeneous, in size, ethos, the socio-economic characteristics of the pupil population including pupil mobility, sector served, degree to which there is a stable, established teaching staff, and so on. It is therefore difficult to replicate home–school initiatives and transplant them from one context to another, as the particular characteristics of both school and parent population and the history of their interaction are crucial in determining the fate of any innovation.

# Key policies and practices

## *Improving teacher–parent communication*

> The teachers can be the dominant partner because they have information parents don't have…. But parents also have lots of information about the children. They may read better at home where they don't feel so pressurised, they may know lots of things the school doesn't even have on its curriculum. I think the problem is getting those bits of your children into the school picture.
>
> (White mother, quoted in Vincent, 1996: 102)

The first point here is to note a difference between information and communication. Some schools send out a great deal of information to parents, but this is not the same as communication, a term suggestive of a two-way process.

Recent research has highlighted the perceptions of many parents that they do not have enough information about the progress made by their individual child, and that it is difficult to engage with that information. The research suggests that parents often find teachers' comments somewhat bland and vague, designed to be reassuring but leaving parents with a residual unease. Many parents have difficulty in 'decoding' 'teacher-speak' (Arrowsmith, 1990; Power and Clark, 2000).

Secondary schools have responded in a variety of ways, bringing them more closely towards practice in primary schools. One of the most noted initiatives is the establishment of student counselling days (also known as academic review days) where instead of a traditional open evening, parents have an individual consultation with their child and the form tutor, who has information from other subject teachers. Progress is discussed and targets are often set. Target-setting has grown considerably in use in recent years. However, its implications and effect on parent, pupil and teacher motivations remain, as yet, an under-researched area. Many schools include short written progress reports in addition to the annual full report (Power and Clark, 2000).

It is clearly important that parents know who to contact as the first port of call (usually the class teacher/form tutor) and how to do this. Several schools are experimenting with voice mail and email for teachers to ease communication between home and school. Innovations in information and communications technology (ICT) are growing. The Bridge Project in the USA has allowed teachers to leave messages in mailboxes for parents to access (Hallgarten, 2000) and some areas (e.g. the London Borough of Tower Hamlets) are piloting projects which fund the electronic linking of home and school. However, in general terms, access to ICT is highly unequal across the social spectrum and this is likely to hinder the spread of developments.

An increasing number of schools produce newsletters to communicate basic information (term dates, etc.) as well as news of achievements and successes. Parents need to be made aware how often such publications should reach them as the 'pupil post' is notoriously unreliable.

A minority of schools in England and Wales – mostly primary schools – hold class meetings. These are designed to provide a meeting point for parents of one particular age cohort and the staff involved, to discuss the year's curriculum and provide a forum for parents and teachers to high-light issues felt to be important, for example homework and/or the school's behaviour policy. Such 'class councils' are common in other European countries such as Denmark and Germany, where they are well established as a mechanism for parent–teacher communication (OECD, 1997). In these countries, parent representatives are elected to provide a link with other parents who cannot attend meetings or to represent the class group on the school council.

A very small number of schools in England and Wales have parents' forums – discussion groups open either to all parents in the school or to class or year group representatives. Such groups have the potential to play an important role in generating dialogue between professional teachers and lay parents. However, since this is an uncommon form of involvement for most parents, such groups are often attended only by those parents who have the confidence and existing knowledge with which to participate. An alternative scenario is that the group is kept by the headteacher within a narrow remit (Martin and Vincent, 1999; Vincent and Martin, 2000).

## Parental involvement in the curriculum

Involving parents with their children's learning, particularly in the early years, is well established and widely accepted across many different countries (OECD, 1997). Home-curriculum schemes, whereby parents are enlisted in working with their children with particular tasks, are more common at the early years and primary levels. These include home-reading (e.g. *Parents and Children and Teachers (PACT); Share*, see Capper, 2000; *Bookstart*, see Wade and Moore, 2000) and home maths (*Into Maths: Parents and Children and Teachers*, see Merttens and Vass, 1993, and Share). Such schemes generally make two main claims. First, that they serve to 'demystify' the teaching process and encourage dialogue between parent and teacher concerning the pupil's learning. Second, that they produce quantifiable increases in children's levels of attainment (e.g. Epstein, 1996). Such claims do have to be treated with some caution, given that they generally derive from relatively short and intense periods of intervention when enthusiasm levels – among parents, teachers and pupils – are at their highest. Furthermore, details of those parents who chose not to get involved are not always forthcoming. Broader criticisms have also been made suggesting that curriculum schemes in effect attempt to make every home function like a primary classroom. Moreover the scope for parents to influence teaching style and content is highly limited despite the climate of openness. Parents are, in effect, co-opted as teacher aides (Brown, 1993; Jowett *et al.*, 1991).

## Parent governors

Parent governors are now a well-established feature of governing bodies in the UK. In England and Wales, governing bodies are also able to co-opt community governors. Secondary schools in particular often use this as an opportunity to bring on board individuals with business or accountancy experience to provide a source of expertise to the governing body as a whole. In England and Wales parent governors are expected to act as 'representative parents', not 'parent representatives'. Despite the innovation of governors' surgeries in a small number of schools, there is often little contact between parent governors and the wider parent body (Deem *et al.*, 1995; Vincent and Tomlinson, 1997).

Each governing body in England and Wales is required to hold an Annual Parents' Meeting and to present a report to parents. These meetings are still affected by low turn-outs, although a growing number of schools are now experimenting with ways of encouraging parents to attend. For example, the event may be linked with an event involving the children (Martin *et al.*, 1995). One multiracial primary school in a recent research study had successfully implemented a discussion-based context for meetings which proved very popular. A topic likely to be of interest to parents was chosen for each meeting (e.g. homework) and after an introduction by the chair of governors and headteacher, parents and governors would discuss the issue in small groups, providing everyone with a chance to comment and hear the opinions of others (Martin and Vincent, 1999).

*Parent accreditation*
Parent accreditation is growing in popularity in England. It involves parents being accredited (by, for example, the Royal Society of Arts, the Open College Network) for work they do supporting children in the classroom and/or making educational games and other materials. Courses usually include an element of adult education. These courses have proved successful with small groups of parents – overwhelmingly mothers – especially in areas of socio-economic disadvantage, where they provide the opportunity for combining knowledge about the development and education of their own children with the opportunity to gain an initial qualification which can increase levels of confidence and provide a way into the workplace or to further education courses (Vincent and Warren, 1998). For example, the home–school curriculum programme *Share* includes an element of accreditation. Other 'parent education' short courses may focus on a range of issues such as behaviour or drugs, and may be run by teachers or outside facilitators using the school's premises.

*Parents as consumers*
The tenor and direction of the restructuring of the education system in the

UK over the last 15 to 20 years has attempted to re-fashion parents as consumers. There is a considerable body of research evidence now that shows that the ability of parents to exercise a consumer role effectively is socially structured (Gewirtz *et al.*, 1995; Whitty *et al.*, 1998b; Hughes and Lauder, 1999). That is, it is professional middle-class parents who have both the capacity and inclination to act as a consumer of education, and operate within the quasi-market to choose a school. However, there is some evidence that many parents value choice even if they do not exercise it, and related to that, an increasing number of parents are becoming aware of their rights and are willing to try to exercise them (Hallgarten, 2000). It seems unlikely that the present choice procedures will be repealed. For the purposes of this chapter, the important point is the relationship between parental choice and voice. Having a choice of school does not necessarily ensure that parents will have a voice within it. Indeed parents are often expected, having made an active consumer choice, to withdraw and leave their children's education in the hands of professionals.

### *Home–school agreements*
Home–school agreements became statutory in England and Wales with effect from September 1999. The agreements set out the rights and responsibilities of parents, teachers and (sometimes) pupils. Every school must have an agreement for parents to sign (although parents do not have to sign and the aspects of the agreement cannot be enforced). Schools were expected to involve at least some of their parent body in consultation about the content of agreements, although there was also central guidance from the Department for Education and Employment (DfEE). Recent research (RISE, 2000) suggests that often schools only consulted with a small number of parents, making the agreement a *fait accompli* for the majority of the parent body and thereby removing any opportunity for dialogue between schools and parents which the creation of the agreements may have offered. The same research also suggests that many teachers and parents are fairly cynical about the usefulness of such agreements. They are seen as largely bureaucratic exercises which cannot

impose good working relationships where these fail to pre-exist between a school and individual families. Agreements have also been criticised for setting out responsibilities for the school which were no more than what is generally required of schools (e.g. helping pupils develop their full potential) while parental and pupil responsibilities tend to be more concrete and specific (RISE, 2000; Vincent and Tomlinson, 1997; Bastiani, 1996; Blair and Waddington, 1997).

## Inter-agency work

Moves towards 'joined-up working' between education and various welfare services are becoming more common in England and Wales. The recent DfEE report, *Schools Plus* (2000a) recommended a network of 'one family support centres', bringing together education, social and health professionals to provide an integrated service for pupils and their families on one site. The proposal is based on the Full Service Schools and New Community Schools of the USA and Scotland respectively (see Chapter 6 for further details). Inter-agency working is integral also to *Sure Start* in England and Wales (DfEE, 2000b) which aims to improve the health and well-being of families and children from birth and during the pre-school years.

## Special education[1]

There are elements of practice and procedure characterising parent–teacher relationships in the field of special education which can provide a model for mainstream practice (OECD, 1997). The nature of pupils' needs and the extra legislative framework within which special education provision is made have both required parents and teachers to work more closely together than is often the case in mainstream relationships. There are two features affecting the home–school relationship within special education which are worthy of note. The first is the existence of parents' groups, mobilising around particular conditions or 'disabilities', but also often forming local umbrella coalitions in order to develop an effective voice in negotiation with the local authority and other local services (Vincent and Tomlinson, 1997; ACE, 1996). A sense of entitlement and confidence tends to vary across the social class spectrum. Professional middle-class parents often have greater resources of social (networks and relationships), cultural (knowledge and skills) and material (goods and finances) capital, with which to formulate and pursue a particular agenda (Riddell *et al.*, 1994). Nevertheless, there are instances (often not fully documented) of local parents' groups developing productive dialogues with service providers in education and health, as well as acting as a source of advice, information and support for individual members (Vincent, 2000).

In England and Wales, all local authorities are now required to have a Parent Partnership Officer (PPO) to steer parents through the process of statutory assessment and recommend sources of independent help and support. A few authorities have chosen to site their PPO in an advice centre setting. Local authority evaluations suggest that these have proved very popular with parents, as well as being effective in mediating between families and schools, and families and the local authority (for example, Wolfendale and Crisp, 1996). This type of liaison/mediation role is also recommended in *Schools Plus* (DfEE, 2000a) where the proposal is for paid Community Learning Champions with a brief to encourage lay adults into the school.

## Evaluation of evidence

Research about parental involvement tends to comprise small-scale local studies and wider generalisations are difficult to draw. This is partly because initiatives in this area are also small-scale and local, and their findings not widely disseminated. As the *Schools Plus* report states about parental, family and community initiatives (for a development of this argument, see also Dyson and Robson, 1999):

> Much of [the research] is reported in the 'grey literature' rather than in more accessible publications, making it more difficult for subsequent research and evaluations to build on earlier findings. Typically evaluations of ... activities were funded by those responsible for the activity and who therefore had a vested interest in the outcomes. These problems

reflect both the bolt-on nature of the provision itself and the lack of commitment or resources to fund longer term evaluations.

(DfEE, 2000a: 78–9)

As noted above, adequate information concerning the target population, and particularly concerning those who do not participate, is often not forthcoming, making informed evaluation or attempts at replication difficult. Thus there is evidence of a certain amount of 're-inventing the wheel' in initiatives in the area of home–school relationships.

Developing home–school and school–community relations more broadly is a medium- to long-term programme, and goals and targets have to be set with that awareness. However, to headteachers feeling under pressure to produce measurable gains in achievement in the short term, the time-span of such a programme can seem unrealistic. Home–school relationships and work with the community then become viewed as an extra, peripheral to the 'real' work of the school, which takes place in the classroom (McClure and Lindle, 1997). Thus it could be argued that there are tensions between the New Labour government's emphasis on standards, which involves the school in narrowing its focus down onto the curriculum, and the school's potentially broader role in combating social exclusion, which requires it to develop links with parents and the wider community.

However, there are a growing number of assertions of the key role played by good home–school relations in relation to pupil achievement and school effectiveness (NCE, 1996; Hallgarten, 2000; Wolfendale and Bastiani, 2000). However, the caveat identified above – that there is confusion surrounding the forms of parental involvement that are the most appropriate, and in particular the forms which impact most positively on pupil achievement – still holds.

The tone of much of the literature in the areas of developing home–school relations is lit with a rosy glow which tends to gloss over any problems and instances of conflict. One key issue that is often subsumed is the question of power (Crozier, 1998), and the imbalances in power between parents and teachers, given teachers' position within an institution and their access to professional expertise. This imbalance can be marked for particular social class and ethnic groups (see also Chapter 3). As a result, the 'partnership' that schools try to encourage often takes place on the professional's terms.

In addition, parents may be offered only a narrow role – that of supporter to and learner from the professional. While access to professional knowledge and expertise can be very valuable to parents both in demystifying the school as an institution and their child's learning, it is not always clear what reciprocal impact parents, particularly socially disadvantaged groups of parents, are allowed to make upon the workings and practices of schools and teachers (Reay, 1998). In response, some parents will reject such an apparently unequal and subordinate relationship, and instead maintain an 'independent' role, with only minimal contact with the school.

## Recommendations

A lack of parental involvement is often perceived to be a problem in schools in areas of socio-economic disadvantage where parents are seen as uncooperative and uninterested. It is possible for schools using the initiatives outlined here to focus on increasing the degree of congruence between the school and home. However such thinking starts from the premise that parents are deficient in a range of ways, and that the focus for change is the home and the family. This one-sided, top-down approach is likely to achieve only limited success. For people to feel a part of an inclusive institution and to feel able to participate, there has to be some mechanism through which they can exercise voice, stating their own views and engaging in deliberation and dialogue with others. The concept of 'voice' focuses the relationship between the school, parents and other adults on debate and conversation. The following recommendations include a review of traditional parent–teacher interactions around individual children, but they also seek to take the relationship further by developing space for lay contributions towards the managing, organising and teaching within schools in the twenty-first century.

Practices of parental and community involvement can be thought of as encouraging one of two types of involvement – individual or collective.

## Individual voice

*   *Communication*
    The vast majority of parents are interested in their child's progress at school. Schools need to review their practices of communication to ensure that they are reaching as many parents as possible and creating the conditions in which parents may be encouraged to engage in a dialogue with the school, concerning the facilitation of their child's learning.
*   *Reporting*
    Are open days/evenings timed to encourage maximum parental partici-pation without completely exhausting the teaching staff? Are parents who do not attend followed up and invited for another appointment? Are open evenings currently the best design or would alternatives (such as consultations with the form tutor) be more appropriate? How many reports on their children do parents receive annually? Are they jargon free, but straightforward in their assessment of the child's progress? Have parents been asked their views on the school's reporting practices?
*   *Other communication*
    The balance between providing parents with informative newsletters and other communications and overloading them with paper is a fine and subjective distinction. Letters and other documents need to be reviewed for their accessibility. Are communications translated when necessary into home languages? Some secondary schools are moving towards practices established in some primary schools where the school produces curriculum booklets, setting out either details of a particular subject programme (at secondary levels), or of the curricu-lum for a particular year (at primary level).
*   *Parental presence*
    Are there opportunities for parents and other adults to come into the school, perhaps to help, but also to see it functioning on a 'normal'

day? It is important, however, given the intensification of work for many of those in paid employment that parental presence is not equated with parental interest.

- *Mediation and development*
Is it possible for a school to appoint someone who can take lead responsibility for developing links with parents and other members of the community? Such an appointee should not become a 'trouble shooter' working only with those families perceived by the school to be problematic. Similarly, a locally-based parents' centre providing advice, information and mediation can offer parents a source of support outside of any one school. Such centres can also provide resources and meeting space for local parent and other community groups, run courses and sell books and other educational materials.

## Collective voice

- *Governors*
Are there any effective links for communication between the governing body and the parent body (e.g. through the parent governors)? Do parents know who governors are? Do governors only communicate with parents in their annual report? Can annual parents meetings be overhauled in any way that will make them seem more attractive and relevant occasions to parents?
- *Forums*
Class/year group councils may be a useful way of encouraging dialogue between school and parents on a variety of issues (e.g. behaviour, homework, and so on). In this they extend beyond traditional parent teacher associations with their remit of fundraising and organising social events. Class meetings, perhaps on a termly basis, provide occasions where parents can meet with other parents and staff to discuss academic and welfare issues relevant to that group of pupils. In a recent research study, we found that the parents of teenage children whom we interviewed missed the opportunities for informal contact that they had with other parents at primary school and would welcome the opportunity

to make links with other parents as well as teachers (Vincent *et al.*, 1999). Class meetings are also opportunities for the teacher to talk about the coming academic programme, and suggest ways in which parents can support their children.

Developing home–school and school–community links requires a huge investment of time, effort and some resources. It is an undertaking that individual schools cannot be expected to make without support from local and central government and other agencies. However, it is a project worth pursuing. Schools have the potential to act as key agents in generating social capital. This term describes the social networks, the shared norms and trust between members of a group and the sanctions that act to deter aberrant behaviour (Putnam, 1995; Halpern, 1999). Social networks may be comprised of 'weak ties' (Granovetter, 1973, cited in Larabee, 1999). Weak ties are those we build with acquaintances, less intense, but usually more wide-ranging in scope than our relationships with close friends and family. Inclusive schools, intent on developing deliberative relationships with parents and other members of the local community, can forge and renew weak ties among a wide range of adults and children, and thereby generate funds of social capital within our society.

## Note

1   The use of the terminology of mainstream and special is not intended to refer only to segregated special education settings, but also to 'special' and 'mainstream' provision within inclusive settings.

# 6 Inter-agency collaborations for inclusive schooling

*Carol Campbell and Geoff Whitty*

There is growing debate that if the purpose of schooling is to become more 'inclusive' and recognise the individual needs of pupils, their families and communities, schools must develop new ways of working with other agencies. A recent review defined 'school inclusion' as encompassing:

> ways in which, and in what circumstances, the involvement of school beyond the conventional boundaries of formal education (as understood in the UK) can generate benefits (however defined) for children/young people, their families and local communities.
>
> (Moss *et al.*, 1999: 1)

Although most schools already provide a range of services and are involved in a range of partnerships, the further development of school-linked inter-agency collaborations has been advocated internationally (see for example, Dryfoos, 1995; Australian Centre for Equity Through Education, 1998; Moss *et al.*, 1999).

The precise nature of such developments and the reasons for their advocacy vary both internationally and within countries. However, in terms of 'inclusive schooling', four key reasons for developing school-linked inter-agency collaboration can be discerned:

1  A pupil's educational achievement cannot easily be separated from their personal, social, emotional and physical development and well-being. Therefore, schools should be aware of, and potentially provide for, children's broader needs. There is an implicit assumption that if children are healthy and happy, their academic attainment will improve, although this is controversial. (A holistic argument.)

2  Furthermore, in contrast to the growing recognition of the holistic and interconnected needs of pupils, existing services and supports are

highly fragmented. Hence, the need for inter-agency collaboration. (A managerial and effectiveness argument.)

3   In addressing the educational and other needs of the 'whole child', schools must be aware of the linkage between pupils, families and local communities. Therefore, school-linked inter-agency collaboration seeks not only to include local agencies but also to include and benefit the local community. (A 'social capital' and 'ecology' argument; see also Chapter 5.)

4   Therefore, there is perceived to be a linkage between school-linked inter-agency collaboration, inclusive schooling and wider processes of social inclusion (although the nature and strength of such a linkage requires further investigation).

The term 'school-linked inter-agency collaboration' is used here to denote a range of activities. First, the focus is on the school. Some critics of school-linked services argue that inter-agency collaboration should be provided at an alternative, arguably more neutral, community base (see for example, Chaskin and Richman, 1993). However, arguments for involving schools include: improved communication between parents and schools; increased community involvement in schools; improved knowledge of students' needs among all relevant agencies; expanded use of already existing, and often under-utilised, school facilities; and improved school attendance (Kadel and Routh, 1993).

Second, the focus is on 'inter-agency' collaborations specifically involving other (public and private) service providers, such as health and social services, rather than on parental involvement or more general community linkages (see Chapter 5 for details of the latter). Third, such collaborations may be either school-linked or school-based. The former may involve agency staff visiting a school or school staff referring pupils to other agencies, whereas the latter involves agencies being located or based in-school. Fourth, there is a range of 'collaborative' activities from those which involve limited co-operation between agencies, to co-location within a school, to full collaboration involving all agencies in planning and decision-making at school level (Crowson and Boyd, 1996a).

## Healthy schools

Internationally, an established and developing form of inter-agency collaboration is for health promotion in schools. In England, however, the notion of the 'health promoting' school (Hamilton and Saunders, 1997) has been superseded by the 'healthy' school, a concept which emphasises 'a reciprocal and potentially synergistic relationship between educational and health goals' (Rivers *et al.*, 1999: 5; see also Aggleton *et al.*, 2000: 102). Writing about government policy in England, Rivers *et al.* conclude:

> By embracing a healthy school philosophy and by actively promoting health through the school environment, curriculum and ethos, as well as through links with parents and local communities, it is hoped that there will be positive impacts on literacy, numeracy and the preparation of young people for citizenship, as well as health inequalities and social exclusion.
>
> (Rivers *et al.*, 1999: 5)

Furthermore, research suggests that education may have an influence (within limits) on wider reductions in health inequalities (Whitty *et al.*, 1998b). Many of the features of 'healthy schools' identified in the National Healthy School Standard (DfEE, 1999), sponsored jointly by the Department for Education and Employment and the Department of Health, are also those of 'effective schools' and 'inclusive schools'.

### *Evaluation[1]*
Between 1998 to 1999, Rivers *et al.* undertook two studies of local healthy schools schemes across England. The first study evaluated the work of eight pilot education and health partnerships in the process of developing schemes. The second study provided an audit of all published and unpublished local evaluations undertaken by existing schemes.[2]

### *Processes*
The research by Rivers *et al.*(1999) indicated that healthy schools worked in partnership with, and received support from, a local scheme. Multi-agency steering or advisory groups contributed to the strategic direction

of a scheme as well as its implementation in schools. The 'more success-ful partnerships had agreed structured systems of working and identified clear roles' (Rivers *et al.*, 1999: 7). The need to develop shared goals and open communication was stressed. Between local schemes and schools, the use of service level agreements was advocated. At school level, the appointment of a member of staff as a co-ordinator of healthy schools activities was vital. Establishing a wider school-based working group was perceived as beneficial to developing a whole school approach, spreading workload and boosting the profile of health-related activities.

There has been considerable debate about which stakeholders to involve and in what ways. The importance of pupil involvement is apparent:[3]

> The view of pupils towards health and its place in the school context could be markedly different from that of the adult interviewees, which underlines the importance of consulting and involving young people in the development of healthy school activities.
>
> (Rivers *et al.*, 1999: 6)

Pupils, across the age ranges, had developed and sophisticated conceptu-alisations of what a healthy school was or should be: it was not concerned simply with narrow health behaviours, such as anti-smoking (although this was not unimportant), but rather an integrated and holistic develop-ment of health, individual well-being and inter-personal relationships. Pupils expected healthy schools to be schools they would enjoy attend-ing, which would stimulate their learning and where they would be respected and listened to by other pupils and staff.

Two main approaches to developing healthy schools were evident:

1  *A needs-led approach* beginning with a baseline audit of existing health-related activities in the school. Subsequently, targets, agreed with the school, were set and future evaluations of progress under-taken.

2  *A prescriptive approach* where criteria were devised by the local healthy schools scheme, in consultation with a multi-agency steering or advisory group.

Rivers *et al.* (1999) do not provide guidance on which approach is preferable. However, there is a need for careful consideration of who is involved in decision-making and in contributing to school self-review or evaluation. Baseline audits provide useful tools for identifying needs and evaluating progress. In developing evaluations, schools require support and there may be a role for an external assessor to ensure rigour and quality. Furthermore, the widespread dissemination of experience and good practice is advocated.

Key processes that were identified as being helpful to the development of healthy schools included:

- staff commitment throughout the school and particularly among senior staff;
- a culture and ethos of supporting health-related activities;
- pupil awareness of and involvement in activities;
- linking health-related activities to the school development plan;
- external financial and other support, including professional development.

Barriers to development included:

- lack of time and resources;
- poor school facilities;
- ineffective communication;
- other pressures on schools and staff, including curriculum reform and inspections.

Evidence from local evaluations of healthy schools schemes suggests that the development of a culture of co-operation and 'partnership working' between agencies that have not been used to working together can pose considerable challenges (e.g. Watkins *et al.*, 2000).

### Outcomes
Nevertheless, the development of a local healthy schools scheme provided a structure for health-related work in schools and raised awareness of such work. Consequently, there was increased motivation in schools to

undertake this work and related policy and curriculum development. Overall, Rivers *et al.* (1999) suggest these activities benefited schools and pupils. For example, in one scheme bullying was less likely to occur and, when it did, it was more likely to be reported. There was a reduction in exclusions and increases in attendance also. While there were not uniform and universal improvements in all health behaviour, there were some improvements from original baseline measures, for example decreased smoking and drug use. An increased use of community links and inter-agency collaboration were evident also.[4]

However, there were some outcomes which proved difficult to reform. Catering contracts, tuck shops and vending machines can create difficulties in ensuring healthy eating. Achieving a 'smoke free' school could be difficult also; this was frequently due to staff smoking. Although staff supported health promotion for pupils, many were reluctant to personally pursue more healthy behaviour.

*Issues*
Both the studies conducted in England, reported above, supported the development of a national healthy schools strategy and informed the substance and the process advocated in the National Healthy School Standard (DfEE, 1999). However, it was important to recognise that 'schools do not come to the scheme as empty vessels' (Rivers *et al.*, 1999: 23), as existing practices need to be recognised, valued and developed. There is a need for support, resources and the continuing professional development of all staff involved. The Standard has attempted to capture this process in school target-setting.

The studies suggest that health-related activities should be linked to school improvement and social inclusiveness, including:

* a whole school approach;
* multi-agency working;
* involvement of pupils in planning and delivery;
* partnerships with parents/carers;
* multi-disciplinary approaches.

There is a need to make the process inclusive of a range of stakeholders, including pupils, and to develop an inclusive approach to health and education, 'which takes account of young people's emotional well-being and issues of race and gender' (Rivers *et al.*, 1999: 57) in curricular developments and health promotion. This approach is now reflected in England's National Healthy School Standard, an important feature of which is the involvement of pupils in the shaping of programme developments.

## Full service schools

In moving to incorporating a wider range of agencies in school-linked activities and developing more 'socially inclusive' schooling, the concept and practice of the full service school has developed in the USA. It should be noted that there are a range of different terms and models in the USA, for example full service schools, extended service schools, community schools and school-linked integrated services (see for example, DeWitt Wallace-Reader's Digest Fund, 1999; Moss *et al.*, 1999). While there are variations between and within these approaches, they share a common focus on developing schooling through extending the scope of provision in schools and developing linkages with other agencies.

Melaville and Blank (1999) categorised the various strategies in terms of 'reform approaches' (see Box 6.1). Their research into 20 of the most widely developed models in the USA revealed that the dominant strategies related to services reform and youth development, although in practice elements of all strategies were combined. There is a need for further research into the extent to which the different principles of reform can be combined in practice. For example, tensions between, on the one hand, effectiveness within schools and, on the other, linkages with communities (Boyd *et al.*, 1997; Kritek, 1996) or tensions between the emphasis on youth development and the importance of the early years (Dryfoos, 1995).

The reasons for advocating school-linked inter-agency collaboration in the USA tend to emphasise the 'needs' of children, society and the economy and the limitations of previous approaches (Boyd *et al.*, 1997).

**Box 6.1** *Reform approaches*

**Services reform**

The services reform approach is grounded in reform efforts within the health and social services sector to provide more efficient and effective services to children and families. Comprehensive service delivery and family support initiatives are designed to knit together the full range of health, family support, mental health and social services. ... Working in tandem with the schools, the primary purpose of these initiatives is to remove the non-academic barriers to improved school performance. The strategy they most often use is to provide access to needed and improved health and human services.

**Youth development**

The youth development approach begins with adolescence and youth development specialists in youth agencies and community centers. ... Schools are valued as environments in which a wide range of opportunities, including relationships with caring adults and positive role models of all ages, may be provided. The primary purpose of youth development is to help students develop their talents and abilities and to participate fully in adolescence and adult life. Its primary strategy is to increase young people's involvement in a wide variety of learning, decision-making, and service activities and to increase constructive interaction with adults and peers.

**Community development**

The community development approach focuses on housing, safety, transportation, and job creation. It emphasizes both physical and economic resource development as well as organizing and mobilizing residents and community leaders and increasing their participation in local decision-making. Schools are viewed as an important forum in which to discuss issues of importance to the community. ... The initial purpose of community development partnerships with the schools is to enhance social, economic and physical capital in school neighbourhoods.

**School reform**

School reform efforts often originate in the schools. ... Efforts have focused both on engaging parents, families and teachers more directly in school-based decision-making and defining and applying high performance standards. Schools have also been receptive to private sector efforts to introduce business efficiency and corporate resources into school management and curriculum. The primary purpose of these initiatives is to improve student achievement. Key strategies are designed to improve school climate and culture, strengthen management and administration, and enhance curriculum and instruction.

*Source:* Melaville and Blank (1999: 4)

In particular, there is a focus on meeting the needs of 'at risk' children, although this terminology is controversial (Moss *et al.*, 1999). Furthermore, there has been some recognition that 'full service schools' may provide benefits to all children and families (Australian Centre for Equity Through Education, 1998). In practice, some school-linked services have eligibility criteria, while others are available to all.

First *et al.* (1993) provided a useful outline of strategies being implemented in different American states. More recently, a national survey of collaborative services by Driscoll *et al.* (1998) in the USA revealed that the most common service provided was 'parenting education' (over 81 per cent of programmes), with 'family support and advocacy' (68.6 per cent) and 'other health education' (67.2 per cent) being second and third most frequently cited.[5] At least 50 per cent of programmes provided a range of basic health services. Driscoll *et al.* (1998) suggest that a 'pedagogical' focus is strong, for example parenting education, tutoring (46 per cent) and/or adult literacy education (over 30 per cent). However, there were examples of school-based but not classroom-oriented services, such as employment-related services (32.8 per cent). Services were generally provided directly at the school. Some of these services were very direct, not simply information generating, for example, the provision of food (51.8 per cent) and child care (53.3 per cent). The number of services provided at schools ranged from 2 to 35, with the average being around 14.

*Evaluation*
There is considerable debate about the evaluation of school-linked inter-agency collaboration. Not all of the local schemes have involved local evaluation from the outset. At the national level, there are difficulties in evaluating the range of different models and approaches, with different goals and objectives serving multiple needs. It can be particularly problematic to evaluate the direct impact of multiple interventions in terms of specific outcomes. Furthermore, many of the initiatives are relatively recent. Current research indicates that it may take at least four years before it is realistic to expect to be able to measure related outcomes (see

Lane, 1998; Zetlin, 1998). Consequently, process evaluations are more prominent at this stage. However, there are the beginnings of outcome evaluations. At the present time, the available evidence must be treated with caution and is inconclusive. There is also a number of evaluations currently underway which may provide useful future information (see Horsch, 1998). The importance of appropriate, rigorous and reliable evaluation at local and national levels have been indicated (Gomby and Larson, 1992; Horsch, 1998).

## *Processes*

Wang *et al.* (1998a) conducted a literature review to identify case study evaluations of collaborative school-linked programmes.[6] Many of the findings relating to the processes of school-level collaboration are similar to those revealed in the healthy schools research. For example: there is a need for senior level support; it is important to include all stakeholders; negotiated written agreements that clarify roles, aims and procedures are helpful; and stable and sufficient funding is necessary.

Given that the average number of services involved is 14, processes can be complex and problematic. There is a need for a clearly identified clientele and defined goals. All the case study sites researched served school children and their families but some provided a wider community function also. The sites tended to have a 'prevention' focus and dealt with multiple needs. It may be most appropriate and desirable to provide 'extended services', which involve schools being open for longer hours and throughout the year (see DeWitt Wallace-Reader's Digest Fund, 1999).

Where relevant, there needs to be explicit discussion of eligibility criteria. There needs also to be agreement about how issues of client confidentiality are to be dealt with between agencies. A common approach was to move towards 'case management':

> Inherent in the concept of school-linked services is the recasting of children's services from the perspective of overcoming children's 'academic', 'physical', or 'physiological' problems to 'cases' of children and families with a variety of needs.
>
> (Wang *et al.*, 1998a: 1)

The use of interdisciplinary teams is important. The extent to which classroom teachers are or should be involved in such teams requires further research. In the case studies, teachers were not always involved, but when they were this produced valuable information for all the professionals. However, the direct involvement of teachers raises questions about job role, workload and professional development.

All of this signifies a potentially considerable change in the purpose, structure and workings of schools. The case studies researched by Wang *et al.* (1998a) indicate that local level developments, rather then top-down mandates, are important for recognising local needs and developing a sense of ownership. It is necessary to develop a new collaborative culture with new norms, rules and a shared vision (see Carlson, 1996). Such processes require ample time and planning. They also require 'technical assistance' (Wang *et al.*, 1998a: 7) involving training. Research has indicated that such training cannot be one-off short courses, but should be part of ongoing continuing professional development and, ideally, incorporated into early professional development, for example in pre-service teacher training (see for example Shaver *et al.*, 1996).

Changes in 'culture' and 'norms' within schools and other agencies are deep-rooted and not straightforward. Research has indicated problems if one agency dominates. Teachers can resist changes and what can be perceived as interference from other agencies. The other professionals can find it difficult to adjust to working in a school. There can be considerable problems of 'turf' and inter-professional conflict. For example, Warren's (1999) case study of school-based youth services found significant 'turf' issues around preserving professional boundaries and autonomous practices. 'Negative turf' arose when responsibilities for difficult practices were passed between agencies, for example was the reporting of a student's suicide the responsibility of the youth service or the school?

There is therefore a need for both strong and shared leadership and a clarification of roles (see Hobbs, 1994; Zetlin, 1998). In seeking to incorporate more services, collaborate with more agencies and extend school hours, there is a need to consider what is desirable and what is feasible.

Included in such considerations are questions about funding and sustainability (Gardner, 1993; Garvin and Young, 1993).

## Outcomes

Wang *et al.* (1998b) undertook a detailed literature search to evaluate outcome measures. They identified a total of 176 outcomes, of which 140 (80 per cent) reported positive results relating to school-linked collaboration.[7] They present their outcome findings relating to the attainment of specific programme goals.

There were a diverse range of outcomes associated with 'integrated services' linking to multiple local goals. Wang *et al.* (1998b: 11) conclude: 'Of utmost importance is the finding that all of the six programs show large numbers of services being provided to children and families in at-risk circumstances'. Another important finding is that integrated services can have a positive impact on teachers. Similarly, an evaluation of the Massachusetts school-linked programme indicated 'very positive effects both on their ability to teach and their effectiveness in working with children' (Market Street Research, 1997: 9). This case study indicated improvements in pupil's self-esteem, behaviour, attendance and academic achievement also. An overview evaluation by Wang *et al.* (1998b: 11) also identified 'positive effects on student's achievement tests, grades, dropout rates, and attendance'.

Research by Wang *et al.* (1998b) indicated:

> Parent education and school readiness have emerged as major school-linked collaborative services. The outcome results for these areas are generally positive also, including improvements in children's readiness for school, parenting skills, maternal development, and the use of community resources.
>
> (Wang *et al.*, 1998b: 9)

In terms of health behaviour and teen pregnancy programmes, outcomes included increased knowledge about pregnancy, reproduction and birth control, plus some decrease in sexual activity. In pregnancy prevention programmes, outcomes included 'delayed age of intercourse, decreased pregnancy rates, and increased use of birth control clinics and contraceptives' (Wang *et al.*, 1998b: 10).[8] However, for both programmes there remained questions about whether, in the long-term, improvements in academic attainment and attendance were maintained.[9]

There were some positive outcomes relating to 'chemical dependency abuse and prevention' goals. Drug use among pupils appears to decrease after participating in chemical dependency programmes. The most successful programmes are those that involve peers. The effectiveness of alcohol programmes is less conclusive. In both cases, the advocated approaches combined information and knowledge about alcohol and drugs, with refusal and coping skills.[10]

In programmes targeting 'dropout prevention', a continuous decrease in 'dropout' from school was noted. Pupils' attendance rates increased and, in most programmes, academic performance and attainment improved. There were 'modest positive effects' (Wang *et al.*, 1998b: 10) on inter-personal behaviour and self-esteem. However, other behavioural outcomes did not improve, for example the rate of suspensions and disciplinary referrals.

In their overall evaluation, Wang *et al.* (1998b) are positive, indicating improvements in terms of specific programme goals and more generally in terms of school-related behaviour, including attendance and achievement. However, there remains debate about the extent to which school-linked inter-agency collaboration can directly impact on student achievement and attainment. For example, based on an evaluation of New Jersey's School-Based Youth Services Programme, Warren (1999: 37) suggested: 'Once students' personal barriers to academic success are removed, it does not automatically follow that their academic problems will simply disappear or be easily removed.' Some programmes provide additional services but do not involve changes in classroom activities or curriculum. From the available evidence, it appears that in order to impact on educational processes and outcomes, school-linked collaboration should involve inter-agency services and have an educational component, ideally linked to curriculum (see for example, Warren, 1999).

## Developing school-linked inter-agency collaboration

Given some 'guarded optimism' (Wang *et al.*, 1998b) about the potential outcomes of school-linked inter-agency collaboration, there have been calls to further develop this concept and practice. However, such developments may differ from current approaches.

Dryfoos (1995) has argued for an expanded version of the existing full service schools model (see Table 6.1):

> My vision of a full service school integrates the best of school reform with all other services that children, youth, and their families need, most of which can be located in a school building. ... Restructured schools attend to individual differences, give staff a wide range of choices regarding teaching methods, organize curricula that are stimulating and relevant, and eliminate tracking and suspensions. The charge to community agencies is to bring the support side into the school: health, mental health, family planning, employment services, child care, parent education, case management, recreation, cultural events, welfare, community policing, and whatever else may fit into the picture. The result is a new kind of 'seamless' institution, a community school with a joint governance structure that allows maximum responsiveness to families and communities and promotes accessibility and continuity for those most in need of services.
>
> (Dryfoos, 1995: 152)

However, it must be noted from previous process evaluations that the creation of 'seamless institutions' will encounter considerable difficulties in early implementation and require ongoing development and support at all levels if they are to become sustainable (Melaville and Blank, 1999). While some studies have indicated significant organisational developments due to inter-agency collaboration (Market Street Research, 1998), evidence tends to indicate that structural changes and reforms of governance and organisation have been limited and slow to develop (Bruner Foundation, 1993; Crowson and Boyd, 1996b; Smithmier, 1997).

Gardner (1993: 190) argued for a move beyond incremental 'add ons' to schools, where 'education reform is what we do inside the classroom

**Table 6.1** Components of full service schools institutions (ideal model)

| Quality education provided by schools | Services provided by schools or community agencies | Support services provided by community agencies |
| --- | --- | --- |
| Effective basic skills | Comprehensive health | Health screening and |
| Individualised instruction | education | services |
| Team teaching | Health promotion | Dental services |
| Co-operative learning | Social skills training | Family planning |
| School-based management | Preparation for the world | Individual counselling |
| Healthy school climate | of work (life planning) | Substance abuse treatment |
| Alternatives to tracking | | Mental health services |
| Parent involvement | | Nutrition/weight management |
| Effective discipline | | Referral with follow-up |
| | | Basic services: Housing, food, clothes |
| | | Recreation, sports, culture |
| | | Mentoring |
| | | Family welfare services |
| | | Parent education, literacy |
| | | Child care |
| | | Employment training/jobs |
| | | Case management |
| | | Crisis intervention |
| | | Community policing |

*Source:* Dryfoos (1995: 152)

and the school; collaboration is what we do outside with other agencies', suggesting this is ultimately ineffective. Furthermore, a move away from the label 'service integration' to focus on 'effective services' is advocated, the former emphasises process whereas the latter focuses on outcomes. Gardner (1993: 193) argued also for recognition of the 'moral imperatives of collaboration' where professionals share responsibility for providing effective services to meet shared goals.

International developments in 'school inclusion' reviewed by Moss *et al.* (1999) indicate the need to consider the purposes of collaboration and the nature of services to be provided. In France, for example, school-linked inter-agency collaboration focusing on issues of citizenship and culture has been developed:

> Social and educational integration is promoted by citizenship studies, from the *ecole maternelle* onwards. Allied to citizenship is an emphasis on culture. Publicly-funded care and leisure facilities outside school hours, including residential holiday opportunities for children. ... Central government money has been provided for local partnerships between schools and local agencies to facilitate children's access to cultural resources and thus their entry to civic life.
>
> (Moss *et al.*, 1999: 10)

These reforms are linked also to changes in the structure of the school day and timetable and to the nature of curriculum.[11] The French example indicates a different purpose and approach to inter-agency collaboration in education.

Criticisms have been made concerning the labelling of 'at risk' students in school-linked inter-agency collaboration in the USA (Moss *et al.*, 1999). Discussions of 'children's needs' which do not take into account children's perspectives have been criticised:

> There is a tendency that 'children's needs' are interpreted from restricting theoretical constructs of what ought to be children's needs, from the viewpoint of psychology. This might in turn lead to a focus on imaginary children rather than attention to real children and their actual as well as theoretical rights.
>
> (Qvarsell *et al.*, 1996: 29)

In Sweden, school-linked inter-agency collaboration is linked to a conceptualisation of children and learning, which emphasises pupils' holistic development. The linkage between schooling, early years services and 'free-time' services for children are well established.[12] This has led to the development of: 'Whole day schools which integrate school classes (either first grades of compulsory school on their own or integrated with preschool classes) with free-time services' (Moss *et al.*, 1999: 28). Although there are variations in the extent of integration in practice, the principle is becoming widespread. Such integration is developed also by the creation of a national curriculum (including goals to aim for and goals to achieve) for schools, pre-schools and free-time services. Staff working with children at all these levels have received university training and there is currently discussion of integrating their training and professional development.

Flising's (1995) study of 59 experiments of integrating school and free-time service in Sweden noted positive developments. Schools and free-time services shared similar concerns to develop children and frequently were working with the same children. While they differed in approach and pedagogy, Flising suggests that their combination enabled a more holistic development of children.[13] However, as with other collaborative approaches, careful attention needs to be given to establishing common management practices, planning, resources, evaluation, support and collaborative cultures.

In particular, Flising (1995) advocates the central role of children in these developments. Moss *et al.* conclude:

> The child is at the centre, a learning child within a learning community, rather than the recipient of already processed knowledge handed down from adults. The processes proposed for the school are seen as relational, based on dialogue between different professionals, between users (children and parents) and professionals, and between users.
>
> (Moss *et al.*, 1999: 35)

Writing about the USA, Honig and Jehl (1999) suggest the need to shift the emphasis in inter-agency collaboration from agencies/services to the needs of individual students. In such a movement, the focus is shifted from inter-agency collaboration to remove barriers to learning to a fuller understanding of collaboration which enables learning.

Honig and Jehl (1999: 7–8) argue that such school-linked collaboration would have five central features:

1 *Focused on whole youth*
  As pupils' 'needs intersect (e.g. poor health affects education affects mental health)' a range of services and supports are provided: 'These services are "comprehensive" not because they include a full range of services but because the services and supports they provide are

appropriate to the needs and strengths of the particular youth of interest to the site.'

2 *Focused on all youth*

Although there may be some targeting of support, it is assumed that all pupils can benefit from services and support.

3 *Youth-centred not organisation-centred*

'The degree of collaboration between organizations is meaningful only to the extent which it improves youths' opportunities to learn.' Collaboration is 'concerned with the coherence of youths' experiences day-to-day rather than the juxtaposition of services and organizations'.

4 *Strengths-based/pro-social*

'Successful strategies are based on the assumption that all youth, schools, and communities have strengths. Such strategies should build on these strengths. Youth are engaged as co-constructors of solutions to their own problems. Deliberate efforts are made to build trust and establish shared values.'

5 *Developmental*

Successful strategies include high expectation of pupils, promoting high standards and supporting pupils to achieve these, rather than being focused on 'fixing problems'.

Honig and Jehl (1999) suggest that such reforms would require changes in the structure and funding of schools. Importantly, they would require developing new relationships between schools and their communities. Briar-Lawson *et al.* (1997) suggest the emphasis on inter-professional collaboration, service integration and systems change are useful developments. However, they argue that these changes in themselves are insufficient to create fundamental improvements in educational outcomes and to create 'inclusive schools'. They propose a 'second generation' of reforms which aim to develop empowering partnerships between teachers, pupils, families and communities, as well as professional inter-agency collaboration (see Crowson and Boyd, 1999; also Chapter 5). The need for pupil involvement and engagement has been stressed (see for example, Moss *et al.*, 1999).

As we have outlined, there are many different purposes for and practices associated with school-linked inter-agency collaboration. Although there have been a number of useful evaluations relating to process issues and positive findings relating to outcomes, such evaluations are still developing and are not conclusive at this stage. As Moss *et al.* (1999: 37) conclude: 'No country has convincing results from evaluations located within the "input-output" paradigm.' Such evaluations may be difficult to achieve given the multiple purposes, processes and goals involved in different forms of inter-agency collaboration. Nevertheless, the development of appropriate local and national evaluations are important.

While there is growing documentation of different models of school-linked inter-agency collaboration, in practice such models have been refined and reformed. In moving from local experimentation to widespread replication and institutionalisation, problems in practice have been discovered (Briar-Lawson *et al.*, 1997). Indeed it may be that various models of inter-agency collaboration are appropriate in different circumstances, reflecting local purposes and needs. In such local developments, the involvement of all stakeholders has been demonstrated to be important, especially for pupils.

However, such local developments are located within wider debates about inclusive schooling and reform. Moss *et al.* argue that we need to develop:

> debates about school inclusion in relation to a wider range of critical questions, not only 'what works?', but also 'who do we think children are?', 'what do we want for our children, here and now (as children) and in the future?', 'what is a good childhood?', 'what is children's relationship to and place in society?' and 'what are the purposes of institutions for children?'
>
> (Moss *et al.*, 1999: 39)

Kirst (1994: 583) suggested that 'education equity needs to be reconceptualised and merged both with the condition of children and a broader conception of children's services than schooling'.

Such arguments suggest that movements towards reforming schools require 'rethinking' the purpose of education, the role of schools and the nature of children (Moss *et al.*, 1999). Furthermore, it requires considering the role and development of teachers. And it requires careful consideration of what 'inter-agency collaboration' should be developed and why, for example targeted services for 'at risk' children, meeting the 'needs' of all children through more inclusive service provision and/or extending the scope and nature of schooling to enable a more holistic development of children and potentially their families and communities.

Importantly, if school-linked inter-agency collaborations are expected to bring about directly, or contribute to, educational improvements, they must be linked to reforms within schools which encourage and enable learning and pupil development.

## Notes

1   'Process' evaluations are essentially formative, for example relating to the introduction and implementation of inter-agency collaboration. 'Outcome' evaluations tend to be summative, emphasising identifiable outputs linked to inter-agency collaboration. Horsch (1998) has indicated the need to develop evaluations of sustainability also.
2   Involving over 2,500 schools in 101 local authorities.
3   Research indicates that pupil engagement is vital to 'inclusive schooling', including anti-sexist and anti-racist developments (see for example, Gillborn, 1995).
4   'One scheme found that scheme schools made more use of outside agencies (using on average six or seven sources) compared with schools not in the scheme who on average utilised three or four' (Rivers *et al.*, 1999: 15).
5   A total of 319 appropriate programmes were identified. Of these, 160 responded to the research survey (a response rate of approximately 50 per cent).
6   From the review, they selected six case studies to represent three key dimensions: (1) single- versus multi-site programmes; (2) publicly versus privately sponsored programmes; and (3) direct service providers versus referral networks. Case #1 was a school district-sponsored, single-site programme. Case #2 was a state-sponsored, multi-site programme. Case #3 was an alternative school, single-site programme. Case #4 was a privately sponsored, multi-site programme. Case #5 was a privately sponsored, single-site programme. Case #6 was a state-sponsored, multi-site programme.
7   Twenty-nine (16 per cent) reported no evidence of change and 7 (4 per cent) reported negative results.

8   The inclusion of sexual health and behaviours advice in school-linked services has resulted in considerable political debate in the USA about whether schools should be involved in providing contraception.

9   Wang *et al.* (1998b) present evidence suggesting that social and behavioural changes may be long term, but more immediate academic improvements may 'fade over time'. Similarly, the findings for 'teen pregnancy prevention and parenting' indicated that while pregnant teenagers receiving support were more likely to stay in school following the child's birth, in the longer term drop out rates were 'comparable to pregnant teenagers who had not been enrolled in the programme' (Wang *et al.,* 1998b: 10).

10  It should be noted that current drugs education has shifted from an emphasis on 'just say no' to drugs awareness and harm minimisation strategies.

11  In addition, there are targeted educational initiatives (zones d'education prioritaires (ZEPs)) in localities characterised by high levels of deprivation.

12  Since 1993, legislation has required the provision of early childhood and free-time services for children aged 1 to 12 years, where these children have particular needs or the parent is employed or studying.

13  According to Moss *et al.* (1999: 29): 'The main work of the school is about teaching and learning "established knowledge", while free-time pedagogy is directed towards supporting development in a broader sense, giving children space and time, and resources for play, creativity, friendships, their own interests and explorations.'

# 7 Effective schools, improving schools and inclusive schools

*Pamela Sammons*

This chapter seeks to set school effectiveness research (SER) and school improvement research in context and examines three aspects: the measurement of effectiveness, the characteristics of effective and improving schools, and the implications for social inclusion.[1]

## School effectiveness and social justice

It is difficult to pin-point the 'start' of SER exactly since many different sub-disciplines have studied schools and classrooms from a variety of perspectives (Creemers, 1994; Reynolds *et al.*, 1994). In the USA and UK, the chief catalyst seems to have been the publication of work by Coleman *et al.* (1966) and Jencks *et al.* (1972). These studies claimed that the particular school attended by a pupil had little influence on their educational outcomes in comparison with factors such as IQ, 'race' and socio-economic status (SES). The focus was thus on structural inequalities rather than on the influence of schools. These studies suffered from limitations and subsequent research has pointed to important school effects while acknowledging the importance of pupil background (Edmonds, 1979; Rutter *et al.*, 1979; Madaus *et al.*, 1979; Willms and Cuttance, 1985; Mortimore *et al.*, 1988; Smith and Tomlinson, 1989).

The last decade has seen a rapid growth in research and in policy and practitioner interest in school effectiveness and its potential as a catalyst for school improvement. Government policy in the UK and elsewhere has sought to draw on school effectiveness and school improvement (SESI) research in attempts to raise educational standards (Barber, 1999). A comprehensive overview of issues in the SER field is provided in the *International Handbook* (Teddlie and Reynolds, 2000).

## Main foci of school effectiveness research

School effectiveness research seeks to disentangle the complex links between the pupil's 'dowry' (the mix of experiences, prior attainments, and personal and family attributes) which any pupil brings to school, from those of their educational experiences at school and to explore the way these jointly influence their later educational attainment, progress and development. The main foci are: the impact of social institutions; characteristics that promote pupils' educational outcomes; and the influence of contexts on outcomes.

SER seeks to provide empirical evidence to assist the evaluation and critique of classroom practice and educational policy (Mortimore *et al.*, 1988; Harris *et al.*, 1995; Sammons *et al.*, 1997; Reynolds, 1997; Gray, 1998; Hill and Rowe, 1998; Mortimore, 1998; Wendel, 2000). The stimulation of reflection, self-evaluation and review can be seen as essential to the development of teachers' professional practice, as well as for instructional development.

The key features of SESI methodology are that it:

- is mainly quantitative, but case studies are important also;
- values reliability and replicability;
- seeks to make generalisations;
- works in partnership with practitioners;
- values views and perceptions of teachers, students and parents.

The use of mainly quantitative methods does not mean that SER is necessarily deterministic or mechanistic in nature. The probabilistic nature of the findings, the need to measure change and the impact of context have been stressed (Teddlie, 1994a, b; Reynolds *et al.*, 1994; Gray, 1998). The subjective views of those involved (pupils, parents or teachers and principals) are seen as vital keys which help to illuminate the way in which school culture can develop and influence both staff and students. Exploring the perceptions of staff and students can be particularly relevant to attempts to engage practitioners in improvement initiatives, as the Scottish *Improving School Effectiveness* project demonstrates (MacBeath and Mortimore, 2000).

## Aims and goals of effectiveness research

Reviewing early SER studies in the USA, Firestone (1991) noted that the effective schools movement was committed to the belief that children of the urban poor could succeed in school (Edmonds, 1979). It was noted also that: 'Effectiveness is not a neutral term. Defining the effectiveness of a particular school always requires choices among competing values' and that the 'criteria of effectiveness will be the subject of political debate' (Firestone, 1991: 2). Early SER research incorporated explicit aims concerned with equity and excellence and focused on the achievement in basic skills (reading and numeracy) of poor/minority ethnic children in elementary schools (Sammons, 1996).

More recent research has moved away from an explicit equity definition towards the study of broader samples of schools and is concerned with the concept of assessing progress over time, rather than cross-sectional 'snapshots' of achievement at a given point in time. This broadens the clientele to include all pupils, not just the disadvantaged. In addition to academic achievement more attention is now paid to social and affective outcomes, for example, attendance, behaviour and self-esteem (Rutter *et al.*, 1979; Mortimore *et al.*, 1988; Smyth, 1999).

SER has provided a powerful critique of raw 'league tables' to monitor school performance and encourage public accountability. The crucial importance of school intake has been increasingly recognised. Attempts to control statistically for intake differences between schools before any comparisons of effectiveness are made is important (Nuttall, 1990; Mortimore, 1991b; McPherson, 1992; Scheerens, 1992; Goldstein *et al.*, 1993; Sammons *et al.*, 1993; Mortimore *et al.*, 1994; Sammons, 1996).

The major flaw in using raw test or examination results to make judgements about school performance is that they take no account of differences between schools in 'the talents and motivations of individual pupils, the nature of their families and communities' (Mortimore *et al.*, 1994: 316). 'Natural justice demands that schools are held accountable only for those things they can influence (for good or ill) and not for all the existing differences between their intakes' (Nuttall, 1990: 25). Exploring the impact of such factors is crucial to attempts to promote social inclusion and widen the social distribution of achievement.

The use of raw 'league tables' of performance can increase pressures on schools to exclude disruptive pupils and encourage schools to take older poor attendees or those unlikely to sit public examinations off role, since these pupils have an adverse impact on raw 'league table' positions (Gray *et al.*, 1999). In value added studies, by contrast, the progress of all pupils counts in evaluating school performance.

The promotion of social inclusion and inclusive schooling requires performance and monitoring systems which are fair to schools serving the most disadvantaged communities and receiving higher proportions of pupils at risk of underachievement. Better ways of identifying and recognising the progress and achievements of these groups of pupils are required without lowering expectations. SER provides models for performance feedback which can provide better estimates of school performance, and especially the potential to focus on effects for different pupil groups.

There are measurement issues surrounding what factors should be included, as controls in studies of school effectiveness remain disputed. It is one matter to demonstrate a statistical relationship between socio-economic status and student attainment, for example, quite another to interpret this relationship. Concern over the possible self-fulfilling prophesy of a culture of low expectations for disadvantaged groups of students remains a vital issue for the promotion of inclusive schools.

### *Definitions of effectiveness*

An effective school is one in which students progress further than might be expected from consideration of its intake (Mortimore, 1991a). An effective school thus adds extra value to its pupils' outcomes in comparison with other schools serving similar intakes.[2] In order to assess value added, measures of an individual pupil's prior attainment are needed to provide a baseline against which subsequent progress can be assessed. Other factors, such as gender, socio-economic status, mobility and fluency in the majority language used at school, have been shown to affect progress also. In addition to prior attainment, SER studies seek to include such factors in assessing the impact of schools.

The need to interpret estimates of an individual school's effects (as in 'outlier' studies of highly effective or ineffective schools) by reference to the confidence limits associated with such estimates is also now widely recognised (Goldstein *et al.*, 1993; Sammons *et al.*, 1994; Thomas and Mortimore, 1996). SER can only distinguish between schools where student progress (or other outcomes) is significantly better or significantly poorer than predicted on the basis of their prior attainment and intake characteristics.

## *Choice of outcomes*

The concept of what constitutes a 'good' school is highly problematic (OECD, 1989; Mortimore and Stone, 1990; Silver, 1994; Gray and Wilcox, 1995). The question of values in education, the purposes of schooling, the quality of pupils' educational experiences remain the subject of much argument (White and Barber, 1997). Critics of SER have claimed that, if the teacher–student learning relationship is 'right', then the educational outcomes will take care of themselves (Elliott, 1996). Against this, the need to gauge learning by measuring its outcomes in some way, and to investigate how these are influenced by teachers' classroom practices and by wider features of school processes over several years, has been argued by SER (Mortimore and Sammons, 1997; Sammons and Reynolds, 1997; Gray *et al.*, 1999).

Rather than attempting to define 'good', and thus by implication 'bad' schools, SER research focuses deliberately on the narrower concept of effectiveness which concerns the achievement of educational goals using specific measures of student cognitive progress, social or affective outcomes. It is argued that effectiveness is a necessary but not sufficient condition for an acceptable definition of a 'good' school.

A broad range of outcomes, cognitive, social and affective, are necessary to provide a satisfactory picture of school effects. Such a range of outcomes is particularly relevant for the promotion of inclusive schools. Evidence indicates that social and affective measures such as attendance, attitudes, behaviour, motivation and self-esteem can act as intermediate outcomes which affect, and can themselves be influenced by, pupils' attainment and progress (Rutter *et al.*, 1979; Mortimore *et al.*, 1988; Louis and Miles, 1992; Lee *et al.*, 1993; Smyth, 1999). Furthermore, school 'connectedness' has been shown to account for 13–18 per cent of the variation in adolescent emotional distress (Resnick *et al.*, 1997).[3] Battistich and Hom (1997) have drawn attention to the relationship between pupils' sense of their school as a community and lower involvement in 'problem behaviours' such as drug use and delinquent behaviour. They conclude that schools that are experienced as communities may enhance students' resiliency.

## Complexity, equity and effective schools

Sammons (1996), Goldstein (1998) and Gray (1998) have drawn attention to *complexity* in the study of school effectiveness.[4] The question of whether schools are equally effective for different groups of students, for example, girls or boys, or those from different socio-economic or ethnic groups, is vital to the concept of inclusive schools. The study of *differential effectiveness* explores such concerns (Mortimore *et al.*, 1988; Tizard *et al.*, 1988; Smith and Tomlison, 1989).

Sammons *et al.* (1997) explored internal variations in secondary schools' academic effectiveness looking at departmental variations in terms of different subjects and for different student groups. It was concluded that effectiveness is best seen as a feature of schools which is both outcome and time specific. For secondary schools, 'effectiveness' needs to be qualified to incorporate both school and departmental effectiveness. Research results also point to the importance of examining trends over time (Gray *et al.*, 1996; Thomas and Mortimore, 1996).

Effectiveness is thus a relative concept dependent on the:

- sample of schools studied;
- choice of outcome measures:
- methodology including adequacy of intake controls;
- time-scale.

Judgements about school effectiveness need to address three key questions essential to consideration of what is meant by an inclusive school and to the promotion of social justice:

1 Effective in promoting which outcomes? – the *what* of effectiveness;
2 Effective for which student groups? – the *who* of effectiveness;
3 Effective over what time period? – the *when* of effectiveness.

## Size of school effects

A number of studies have sought to quantify the size of school effects. A systematic meta-analysis is reported by Scheerens and Bosker (1997). They conclude that net effects (after control for intake) are larger for mathematics than language, and largest for studies based on composite measures of achievement. On average schools accounted for 8 per cent of the achievement differences between students after control for initial differences. This research also indicates that classroom level or teacher effects tend to be substantially larger than school effects (see also: Rowe and Hill, 1994; Hill and Rowe, 1998). Teacher effects emerge more strongly in studies conducted across one school year and in primary school studies.

Scheerens and Bosker (1997) conclude that the relatively modest size of estimated school effect should not be downplayed given the average impact a school has on all its students. They note that, technically, effect sizes should be considered in relation to the number of students in the school in a given year or the number of students leaving the school over a period of years.

Using particularly detailed information about pupils' background characteristics, Sammons *et al.* (1993) demonstrate that, *in total*, background factors (age, gender, ethnicity, fluency in English, entitlement to free school meals (FSM), and parents' occupational status) taken together account for 20.6 per cent of total variance in primary pupils' reading scores in year five and for mathematics the figure is lower at around 11 per cent. In this study the school effect was found to account for 8–9 per cent of the total variance in these outcomes.

A further way of considering the size of school effects is to consider the difference between outliers (significantly more or less effective schools) on student attainment in public examinations. Thomas and Mortimore (1996) show that, for a student of average prior attainment at age 11 years, the difference in total GCSE points score was 14 points (equivalent to the difference between obtaining seven grade B or seven grade D GCSEs) between the most and least effective schools. In the *Improving School Effectiveness* study in Scotland, the difference reported was equivalent to six Standard Grades at Grade 3 rather than six at Grade 4 (MacBeath and Mortimore, 2000); Grade 3 has been seen as the usual cut off for progression to Scottish Highers and hence entry to higher education or advanced further education.

## Differential effects and equity issues

The question of whether school effects differ between specific groups of pupils is of critical importance to the promotion of inclusive schooling. Sheerens and Bosker argue that: 'Schools matter most for underprivileged and/or initially low achieving students. Effective or ineffective schools are especially effective or ineffective for these students' (Scheerens and Bosker, 1997: 96).

It must be stressed that SER does not suggest schools can, by themselves, overcome social disadvantage (Mortimore and Whitty, 1997). Nonetheless, attending an effective school can have a powerful impact. Research by Mortimore *et al.* (1988) on primary school influences on progress over three school years illustrates that working-class pupils attending the most effective schools made greater progress and had higher attainment at the end of the study than middle-class pupils in the least effective schools. Within the most effective schools however, middle-class children as a group continued to outperform their working-class peers, reflecting their initial higher starting point. Furthermore, Mortimore and Whitty (1999) suggest that in effective schools generally, the relative advantage of middle-class pupils may actually increase. There is therefore considerable debate about the differential effectiveness of schools, with some studies indicating particular benefits of school effectiveness for pupils with low socio-economic status, low prior attainment and/or minority ethnic pupils (see for example: Nuttall *et al.*, 1989; Bryk and Raudenbush, 1992; Sammons *et al.*, 1993; Bosker, 1995; Thomas *et al.*, 1997). However, while overall improvements may benefit all, resulting in absolute improvements in attainment, this does not necessarily result in relative improvements for disadvantaged groups. The nature of differential effectiveness and the potential of school effectiveness to benefit disadvantaged pupils are important to the development of inclusive schooling.

## Understanding effectiveness

To what extent can SER illuminate the black box of how school and classroom experiences combine to foster or inhibit student progress and their social and affective development? This forms the crucial intervening link in the input/output models used to identify school effects by controlling for intake differences in pupils' prior attainment and background characteristics.

An important question concerns the generalisability of SER findings and the extent to which they can be used by those engaged in school improvement (see Reynolds *et al.*, 1994). A number of reviewers have identified common features concerning the processes and characteristics of more effective schools (e.g. Purkey and Smith, 1983; United States Department of Education, 1986; Reid *et al.*, 1987; Gray, 1990; NWREL, 1990; Firestone, 1991; Riddell and Brown, 1991; Mortimore, 1991a, b, 1995a, b).

A synthesis of reviews by Scheerens and Bosker (1997) distinguished the following set of general factors:

- productive climate and culture;
- focus on central learning skills;
- appropriate monitoring;
- practice-oriented staff development;
- professional leadership;
- parental involvement;

- effective instructional arrangements;
- high expectations.

They conclude:

> This agreement amongst reviewers from different countries, who have sometimes concentrated on different kinds of effectiveness-oriented studies, points to the existence of an international agreed-on 'educated' common sense on 'what works' in education.
>
> (Scheerens and Bosker, 1997: 207)

Teddlie and Reynolds (2000) mapped the relationships between the correlates of effectiveness identified by Levine and Lezotte (1990) in the USA and by Sammons *et al.* (1995) in the UK, and distilled the findings into nine process areas (Table 7.1).

Nevertheless, the probabilistic nature of SER findings has been highlighted:

> As a rule, schools which do the kinds of things the research suggests make a difference, tend to get better results (however these are measured or assessed). The problem is these are tendencies not certainties. In betting terms the research would be right about seven out of ten times, especially if it could be supported by professional assessments.
>
> (Gray, 1990: 214)

*Ineffective schools*

Gray and Wilcox argue that: 'How an "ineffective" school improves may well differ from the ways in which more effective schools maintain their effectiveness' (1995: 2). Stoll and Fink (1996) reviewed studies concerning the characteristics of ineffective schools and highlight four aspects:

1 lack of vision;
2 unfocused leadership;
3 dysfunctional staff relationships;
4 ineffective classroom practices.

**Table 7.1** *The processes of effective schools*

| | |
|---|---|
| **1 The processes of effective leadership** | Being firm and purposeful; Involving others in the process; Exhibiting instructional leadership; Frequent personal monitoring; Selecting and replacing staff. |
| **2 The processes of effective teaching** | Unity of purpose; Consistency of practice; Collegiality and collaboration. |
| **3 Developing and maintaining a pervasive focus on learning** | Focusing on academics; Maximising school learning time. |
| **4 Producing a positive school culture** | Creating a shared vision; Creating an orderly environment; Emphasising positive reinforcement. |
| **5 Creating high (and appropriate) expectations for all** | For students; For staff. |
| **6 Emphasising student responsibilities & rights** | Responsibilities; Rights. |
| **7 Monitoring progress at all levels** | At the school level; At the classroom level; At the student level. |
| **8 Developing staff skills at the school site** | Site based; Integrated with ongoing professional development. |
| **9 Involving parents in productive and appropriate ways** | Buffering negative influences; Encouraging productive interactions with parents. |

*Source:* After Teddlie and Reynolds (2000)

Ineffective classroom practices were seen to be characterised by: inconsistent approaches to the curriculum and teaching; generally lower expectations for students of low SES; an emphasis on supervising and communicating about routines; low levels of teacher–pupil interaction; low levels of pupil involvement in their work; pupil perceptions of their teachers as people who did not care, praise, provide help, or consider learning as important; and more frequent use of criticism and negative feedback.

The importance of school culture is highlighted by Reynolds (1995: 61): 'the ineffective school may also have inside itself multiple schools formed around cliques and friendship groups ... there will be none of the organisation, social, cultural and symbolic tightness of the effective school.' Such tightness appears to be a particular requirement for academic effectiveness in the context of the inner city.

### The centrality of teaching and learning

A number of SER authors have drawn attention to the centrality of teaching and learning, and of classroom processes in determining schools' academic effectiveness (Creemers, 1994; Scheerens and Bosker, 1997; Hill and Rowe, 1998). Sammons *et al.* (1995) argue that the quality of teaching and expectations have the most significant role to play in fostering students' learning and progress and, therefore, in influencing their educational outcomes. Given this, school processes, including leadership, remain influential because they provide the overall framework within which teachers and classrooms operate. In some schools (those that are more effective) the overall framework is more supportive for student learning and classroom practice. SER suggests that school-level conditions and leadership are particularly relevant influences on effectiveness and improvement in schools serving socio-economically disadvantaged pupils.

Reviews of teacher effectiveness literature have identified a number of characteristics of effective teachers (after Joyce and Showers, 1988):

• they teach the class as a whole;
• they present information or skills clearly and animatedly;

- they keep the teaching sessions task-oriented;
- they are non-evaluative and keep instruction relaxed;
- they have high expectations for achievement (give more homework, pace lessons faster and create alertness);
- they relate comfortably to students (reducing behaviour problems).

The Hay McBer (2000) report seeks to develop a model of teacher effectiveness which links three factors (professional characteristics, teaching skills and classroom climate) to pupil progress. The report suggests that over 30 per cent of the variance in pupil progress can be predicted by these three factors. The teacher's role in creating an 'excellent classroom climate' is stressed. In primary schools, outstanding teachers scored more highly in terms of behaviours related to high expectations, time and resource management, assessment and homework. At the secondary level, the biggest differences were in high expectations, planning and homework. Hay McBer (2000) identify three factors as significant to pupils' learning opportunities in the classroom:

1  lack of disruption;
2  encouragement to engage;
3  high expectations.

### Structured teaching

The features of 'structured teaching' have been identified (Scheerens, 1992) as particularly relevant to promoting cognitive attainment in the basic skill areas especially in schools serving higher proportions of socio-economically disadvantaged pupils. Characteristics of structured teaching include (after Scheerens, 1992):

- making clear what has to be learnt;
- splitting teaching material into manageable units for pupils and offering these in a well-considered sequence;
- exercise material in which pupils make use of 'hunches' and prompts;
- regularly testing for progress with immediate feedback of the results.

Stringfield *et al.* (1994) have drawn attention to the need for special strategies, particularly the benefits of high expectations and structured teaching, for disadvantaged pupils. Curriculum coverage has also been shown to be important. In a study of ethnically diverse inner city schools, Plewis (1998) shows that, controlling for prior attainment and background, curriculum coverage was an important predictor of young pupils' mathematics progress.

## School, departmental and classroom effectiveness

The SER field has developed models of educational attainment which attempt to demonstrate the nature and direction of links between particular school processes and student outcomes. The framework of input–process–output has been commonly adopted, and the importance of context has also been widely recognised (Teddlie, 1994a; Brown *et al.*, 1996).

There has been an increasing recognition also of the importance of classroom/teacher effects in SER and attempts to utilise three level models to separate school, class and pupil effects (Rowe and Hill, 1994; Luyten, 1994, 1995; Hill and Rowe, 1996). Within a school, students will experience a succession of teachers and classes. However, it is important to recognise that students usually spend several years in one institution and therefore the question of whether over several years the particular school attended has an impact on their later educational outcomes remains of prime importance for the promotion of social inclusion.

SER research indicates that schools are best studied as organisations which are made up of nested layers – students within classrooms, departments within schools. The most pervasive view on cross-level influences in nested (i.e. multilevel) models of school effectiveness is that higher level conditions (aspects concerning school leadership, policy and organisation, for example) in some way facilitate conditions at lower levels (the quality of teaching and learning in classrooms) which, in turn, have a direct impact on pupils' academic outcomes (see: Goldstein, 1987; Scheerens and Bosker, 1997; Hill and Rowe, 1996, 1998). Bosker and Scheerens (1994) highlight various possible ways school-level processes may affect classroom practice.

On the basis of their empirical research, Sammons *et al.* (1997) concluded that models of secondary school effectiveness need to analyse the impact of the department explicitly.[5] Their results showed that, in the majority of cases, secondary schools cannot be readily classified as either clearly effective or clearly ineffective. The concept of secondary school effectiveness needs to be qualified to the term school and departmental effectiveness.

The research also pointed to the adverse impact of high levels of staff absence in the school or specific departments, and of shortages of qualified teachers. Staff shortages and high levels of absence inevitably affect the quality of teaching in individual classrooms and in departments teaching specified subjects (e.g. mathematics, science or languages in which the supply of qualified teachers has been problematic for many schools in inner-city areas). However, high levels of staff absence and difficulties in recruitment/retention of good teachers may also be a symptom as well as a cause of academic ineffectiveness, being influenced by staff morale and by school and departmental leadership.

The creation of a positive school culture based on the knowledge derived from SER can be viewed as a potential focus for school improvement initiatives, requiring the participation and commitment of staff, students and parents (Scheerens, 1992; Wendel, 2000). Sammons *et al.* (1997) point to the importance of school and departmental ethos or culture in determining the academic effectiveness of secondary schools (see also Smyth, 1999).

The key aspects of an effective school and departmental culture include (Sammons *et al.*, 1997):

* order – behaviour, policy and practice;
* academic emphasis;
* student-focused approach.

An effective school manages to achieve an optimal balance between the social control task achievement and the expressive social cohesion domains, according to Hargreaves (1995). Behaviour policy and practice, leading to a safe orderly working environment and an academic emphasis are necessary for task achievement (effective teaching and learning and thus students' academic progress), while the student-focused environment concerns social cohesion and creates a positive climate for learning.

In their review of effective secondary schools in the USA, Lee *et al.* (1993) found evidence that schools with a common sense of purpose and a strong communal organisation (involving collegial relationships among staff and positive adult–student relationships) are effective in promoting a range of student academic and social outcomes reflecting pupil engagement and commitment. They stress the importance of pupils' and staffs' experience of the school as a social organisation and the quality of human relationships experienced within it:

> it is clear to us that 'good' or 'effective' schools must couple concern for social relations with an appreciation for the structural and functional aspects that instrumentally affect instruction and academic learning.
>
> (Lee *et al.*, 1993: 228)

In Hong Kong, Ming and Cheong's (1995) research drew attention to the benefits of a caring and supportive climate and a cohesive student-centred philosophy of teaching for the entire school. Reynolds (1995) draws attention to the importance of school-level socialisation processes. The achievement of a positive and consistent school culture appears to be crucial for effectiveness. This finding is especially relevant to the creation of inclusive schools.

## Implications for school improvement

School improvement has been defined as 'a strategy for educational change that enhances student outcomes as well as strengthening the school's capacity for managing change' (Hopkins, 1994: 3).

It is important to recognise that SER does not claim to provide a simple or universal blueprint for improvement (Reid *et al.*, 1987; Mortimore *et al.*, 1988; Creemers, 1994; Sammons, 1994). School improvement efforts require a particular focus on the processes of change and understanding of the history and context of specific institutions (Louis and Miles, 1991;

Fullan, 1991, 1993; Stoll and Fink, 1994; Gray *et al.*, 1999; Joyce *et al.*, 1999; MacBeath, 1999a, b)

West and Hopkins (1996) have drawn attention to the need to reconceptualise both school effectiveness and improvement. They draw attention to an over-emphasis on the potential of managerialist solutions to the problems of so-called ineffective schools. In their critique of school improvement, they note the tendency for many projects to focus on teachers' perspectives and concerns and on the potential of staff development, while frequently *avoiding* the question of impact on student learning and outcomes. West and Hopkins (1996) propose a more comprehensive model for the effective school which focuses on four domains: student achievements; student experiences; teacher and school development; and community involvement.

Hillman and Stoll (1994) identify ten key processes for school improvement:

1 clear leadership;
2 developing a shared vision and goals;
3 staff development and ongoing teacher learning;
4 involvement of pupils, parents and the wider school community;
5 use of an evolutionary development planning process;
6 redefining structures, frameworks, roles and responsibilities;
7 emphasis on teaching and learning;
8 monitoring, problem solving and evaluation;
9 celebration of success;
10 external support, networking and partnership.

Leithwood and Louis (1999) argue that school restructuring and reform should support teaching and learning and focus on the students' experience of education more directly, with schools becoming 'learning organisations' (see also MacGilchrist *et al.*, 1997).[6]

*Evaluation*
Many school improvement initiatives have been criticised for limited approaches to evaluation. The evaluation of such initiatives requires the

development of adequate baseline measures prior to the introduction of changes, as well as collection of information during the course of a project in order to gauge likely impacts on a range of relevant outcomes. Creemers and Reezigt (1997) point to the need for sustained interactivity between school effectiveness and better attempts to test different school improvement strategies to evaluate their impact.

Of particular relevance to the promotion of social inclusion are evaluations of improvement initiatives in socio-economically disadvantaged urban areas.[7] Barber and Dann (1996) highlight a number of strategies which, when used in combination, were identified as contributing to school improvement. These included:

- changing the head;
- providing external consultancy;
- changes in the staff;
- changing the culture;
- learning networks;
- greater openness about performance information;
- an agreed constructive approach to pupil discipline;
- an effective staff development policy related to the school's overall development strategy.

An example of an evaluation of a school improvement initiative which sought to build on the SER knowledge base is provided by Taggart and Sammons (1999). This used a range of sources of evidence in evaluating the impacts of the three-year *Making Belfast Work Raising School Standards* project which involved secondary schools identified as having low attainment, poor attendance and serving highly disadvantaged communities. Factors which assisted improvement were identified as well as barriers to success. The development of schools' capacities for action planning, monitoring and evaluation, substantial extra resources, and the benefits of staff and curriculum development and collaboration between schools were noted. Barriers included the relatively short (three-year) time-scale, hurried start leading to rushed plans in year one, lack of advice on baseline measures, and the public naming of secondary schools

as lowest achieving institutions in the press at the start of the project leading to low staff morale.

Prior attainment and socio-economic factors are two of the major
influences on student attainment and progress as shown by SER. Case
study and questionnaire evidence from the *Improving School Effectiveness Project* in Scotland (Robertson and Toal, 2000) also suggests that
teachers' attitudes and perceptions are associated with these same influences; that teachers' views of the quality of their schools are significantly
associated with factors other than value-added status. Robertson and Toal
(2000) conclude that value added is not a concept that has significantly
permeated the perceptions of teachers. Stronger influences are those well
established in the history and ethos of schools and in the nature of their
pupil population, especially socio-economic factors. This has important
implications for school education and inclusiveness. Generally, teachers'
views of school quality match the attainment level of the school. This
would suggest that in schools faced with the challenges of low prior attainment and socio-economic disadvantage, additional obstacles to improvement might be low teacher expectation and generally low morale.[8] If
schools are to make continuing improvements in pupil achievement,
these issues of staff attitude and expectation (which relate to the concept
of school culture) require greater attention, particularly in disadvantaged
and low attaining schools.

There is growing agreement that to promote improvement schools
should address 'proximal variables' like curriculum, instruction and
assessment which emphasise student outcomes. Muijs and Reynolds
(2000) report the results of a recent primary school improvement project
which focused explicitly on teachers' classroom practice in relation to
mathematics teaching. The Gatsby project used a quasi-experimental
design and found clear differences between experimental and control
school teachers on nine measures of teacher behaviour. Pupil progress
was significantly higher in project classes, the most significant factors
were effective interactive teaching, direct instruction and varied teaching.
The authors examined the relationship between pupil progress and
teacher behaviours in relation to the proportion of pupils' level of prior

attainment, and those disadvantaged as measured by FSM. They found that the benefits of interactive whole class teaching were greater in classes where there were higher proportions of low ability and disadvantaged students. They conclude that structured teaching methods are most effective for teaching basic skills and that more disadvantaged pupils benefit most from such approaches at the primary level. They also note that boys seem to benefit from the use of interactive whole class teaching.

### Schools 'causing concern'

Gray (2000) analysed challenges faced by schools identified as 'causing concern'. He concludes that schools removed from special measures in England appear to improve on the quality of teaching, attendance (especially in secondary and special schools) and reduction in exclusions. Improvements in attainment were less evident and may take longer to become apparent. Gray observes that change is more likely where parents and governors are involved, and where the need for change is accepted by both staff and pupils. He also notes that change is more likely in schools where there is an absence of extreme social deprivation and where the history of problems at the school is relatively short. These latter conclusions are particularly relevant to inclusive schooling.

### School restructuring

In the USA, Stringfield (1994) has argued that schools need to evolve into high reliability organisations (HROs), particularly in relation to the education of 'at risk' and disadvantaged pupils. Stringfield *et al.* (1996) provide a detailed analysis of the impact of nine New American School development teams which sought to create and implement whole school restructuring designs. They conclude:

> A general lesson for all school reform is that teachers cannot operate effectively to change classroom behaviours without concrete supports to guide their efforts, and time to learn and assimilate new behaviours. Schools cannot hope to accomplish the changes envisaged by the designs, unless the implementation strategy supports all the staff and enables them to work together toward reform. ... Long term commitment

by teachers was developed over time in a working relationship where a team and a school staff interacted with each other towards common goals. Strong assistance toward change, concrete models, coaching, and time produced change and, therefore, more commitment.

(Stringfield *et al.*, 1996: 320)

The effectiveness of design-based programmes was found to be related to the following strategies (Stringfield *et al.*, 1996):

* A capable design team that could provide design-related assistance to multiple sites. A fully developed design that should communicate effectively the vision and specific tasks of school reform advocated by the team. This design should include a regular self-assessment by the school to feed back information useful in measuring the school's progress toward reform and to provide guidance for areas of improvement.
* A proven implementation strategy that allows schools to become adept at quality control of the curriculum and instruction, and aids schools in changing the structure of professional development, scheduling and governance to support student education goals.
* The existence of demonstration sites to act as further laboratories of reform and to provide hands-on evidence of success.

*Evaluation of specific initiatives intended to combat social exclusion*
Riley *et al.* (2000) provide a summary of initiatives designed to address pupil disaffection. Initiatives which appeared to be working most effectively were aimed at:

* Improving relationships between pupils and teachers;
* Changing schools' and teachers' practices, including increased opportunities for greater teacher collaboration, more individualised approaches to particular pupils, and use of innovative teaching methods and styles;
* Increasing the level of support within schools; for example, school-based counselling programme, peer counselling and homework support;

• Providing pupils with a more encouraging and realistic view of the future; for example, extended work experience and programmes helping pupils to identify their own strengths and weaknesses.

## Other approaches

It is beyond the scope of this review to examine the role of inspection evidence in relation to school improvement which has taken different routes in Scotland in comparison with England (for discussions see: Matthews and Smith, 1995; McGlynn and Stalker, 1995; Earley *et al.*, 1996; Wilcox and Gray, 1996). Likewise, the national literacy and numeracy strategies in England and Wales require further investigation, particularly in their impact on disadvantaged and vulnerable groups. Both strategies drew on school and teacher effectiveness research in developing their approaches. In light of USA evidence by Slavin (1996) it might be expected that such approaches would be of particular benefit to disadvantaged groups. For example Ross *et al.* (1999) report that the 'Success for All' programme was particularly beneficial in promoting the reading attainment of African American students and the sub-sample of lowest 25 per cent of initial attainers. Careful monitoring will be required to explore this issue in relation to the impact of national literacy and numeracy strategies. It is possible that achievement levels of disadvantaged groups improve but at a different rate from that of more advantaged groups. This could lead either to a decreased or to an increased performance 'gap'; while in both cases better standards overall and for disadvantaged pupils would be found.

Other relevant UK policy developments have sought to build on the potential benefits of providing schools with better performance data using contextualised approaches. The Autumn Package (first sent to all schools in England in 1998) is intended to form part of the DfEE's five-stage model of the improvement cycle. In contrast to raw 'league tables' the provision of data is not published at the school level but is sent to schools to facilitate internal school self-evaluation and development planning. The Package encourages monitoring the progress of different pupil sub-groups and provides schools with contextualised performance and inspection information related to schools with similar profiles in terms of prior attainment and social disadvantage of intakes. It also advocates target-setting for individual pupils and for different sub-groups.

The positive impact of pre-school and early years interventions such as Reading Recovery is likewise beyond the scope of this review (for a summary see Sylva *et al.*, 1999). Interim results from the five-year Effective Provision of Pre-school Education project funded by the DfEE indicate that pre-schools can have a positive impact on young children's cognitive progress and social behavioural development by school entry. The research indicates that pre-schools do not eliminate but can help to reduce the powerful influences of social disadvantage already evident in children's cognitive development at age 3 years plus (House of Commons Education Sub-Committee Early Years Inquiry, Minutes of Evidence, 21 June 2000).

## Criticisms of school effectiveness research

The growing field of SER has received criticism from a number of quarters in recent years. Examples of criticisms and responses to these include Hamilton (1996: 56) who argued that the field has become an international industry and should be seen as 'an ethnocentric pseudo-science that serves merely to mystify anxious administrators and marginalise classroom practitioners'. Likewise, Elliott (1996) claims that SER exhibits 'a mechanistic methodology, an instrumentalist view of educational processes and the belief that educational outcomes can and should be described independently of such processes' and is 'underpinned by values which are anti-educational' and that its findings 'tell us nothing new about schools'. He concludes that 'they are best viewed as ideological legitimisations of a socially coercive view of schooling' (Elliott, 1996: 200).[9]

The criticisms of SER can be classified under a number of headings:

- *Political/philosophical*
  It is suggested that SER supports conservative and market forces ideology and marginalises equity issues.
- *Methodological*
  Critics commonly exhibit a strong distrust of quantitative approaches to research and, in particular, are against the measurement of student outcomes, favouring action research and a focus on processes and values instead.
- *Theoretical*
  Critics accuse the field of being a-theoretical, are against the use of input–process–output models and attempts to study statistical associations and causality. Some claim that SER findings tell us nothing new about schooling and are just 'common sense'.

Teddlie and Reynolds (2001) provide a defence of SER by drawing attention to a number of limitations in the scope of some critics' engagement with the SER field. They claim that SER will always be politically controversial because it concerns the nature and purposes of schooling and suggest that critics have often made contradictory claims about the field. For example, SER research has been criticised by 'conservatives' in the US during the 1980s and since the late 1990s in the UK (e.g. by former Her Majesty's Chief Inspector of Schools in England, Chris Woodhead) for its 'liberal' agenda, the attention given to minority ethnic and low SES students, the focus on schools in inner city contexts and the stress given to the power of intake in studies of school performance. By contrast, 'progressive' critics in the UK perceive SER as giving credence and legitimisation to a conservative ideology and lack of attention to 'values' in education. In countering the claims of critics Teddlie and Reynolds (2001) stress that:

- SER is *not* the underpinning for educational policy in most countries;
- SER is *not* the dominant field in educational research and policy making in most countries (in the UK in fact researchers in the field have been strong critics of market policies and of a raw 'league tables' approach to raising standards from 1988 onwards);

- SER *does* take into consideration context factors, contrary to the claims of some critics.

Teddlie and Reynolds also note the wide diversity of SER approaches and developments that have taken place. It is argued that there are three distinct major strands to SER:

1 School effects research – focus on measurement and identification of differences;
2 Effective schools research – focus on processes of effective schooling, often uses 'mixed methods';
3 School improvement research – focus on educational change, actively involves practitioners.

They suggest also that there are three main types of researchers in the field – scientists, pragmatists and humanists – and thus accusations that the SER field is homogenous and has a well-defined political agenda, reflect a simplistic and narrow reading.

## The impact of SES

The extent to which SER addresses the impact of socio-economic status is crucial to the consideration of its implications for a review of inclusive schooling. Critics such as Thrupp (2001) argue that SER has ignored, or downplayed, the impact of social class while overstating the importance of schools. As noted earlier, many SER studies have drawn considerable attention to both the impact of the individual pupil's social class background and that of the SES mix of the student body in the school the pupil attends.

There are indeed important group differences in average achievement levels related to factors such as social class at all stages in education, but also considerable overlap (i.e. much greater variation within than between social class or income groups). Aggregate analyses by social class group thus ignore the extent of variation at the level of the individual pupil (the ecological fallacy). The multilevel methods of analysis adopted in SER allow the separation of variation in pupil attainment and progress related to the teaching group, the school and the impact of particular pupil characteristics such as SES or gender for example. It has been shown that factors such as social class and income (e.g. using parental occupation and the FSM indicators) are poor predictors of any individual pupil's attainments. Nonetheless, these factors account for much of the difference between schools in their overall results. Hence the importance of adequate intake control in SER studies, both in terms of the individual pupil's characteristics and those of the intake group as a whole (see Mortimore *et al.*, 1988; Smith and Tomlinson, 1989; Sammons *et al.*, 1995). Critics overstate the size of social class relationship compared with that of the school or teaching group (reflecting their reliance on the use of simple aggregate statistics).

Teddlie and Reynolds (2001) conclude that:

- SER shows that schools do have an impact beyond that of social class and are interested in practical applications to promote all students' achievements;
- Researchers in the field believe that educators should try to influence what happens in their schools and classrooms rather than focusing only on the supposed 'limitations' of student background and society.

In considering the contribution of SER, Mortimore (1995a) reaches a number of conclusions about its impact including that SER has:

- moderated over-deterministic sociological theories about home and background;
- qualified an over-reliance on psychological individualistic theories of learning;
- focused attention on the potential of institutional influences;
- provided, as a result, a more optimistic view of teaching and renewed attention to learning concerns as well as on school management;
- advanced the methodology of the study of complex social effects;
- stimulated many experiments in school improvement;
- contributed to a growing set of theoretical ideas about how pupils learn in particular school settings.

An illustration of the consideration given to the impact of SES context on schools' performance and the implications for educational policy and the promotion of inclusion is given in the *Forging Links* study of variations in secondary school and departmental effectiveness in inner London. This study concluded that:

> The challenges faced by schools in socio-economically disadvantaged areas require serious recognition. Ways of improving such schools' attractiveness to teachers need to be developed. Current policies – such as the publication of raw league tables – are likely to add to staff demoralization in such areas. This tends to discourage teachers from applying for jobs in these schools because of the risk of association with institutions which are more likely to be identified as 'failing' or requiring special measures. The rewards for headteachers in such schools also need to be improved. ... Although resources are certainly not the answer to all educational problems, ways of ensuring that inner city schools can attract and retain good staff at all levels need to be identified and given a high priority.
>
> (Sammons *et al.*, 1997: 188)

## School effectiveness, school improvement and inclusive schooling

In his analysis of the positive effects of schooling, Mortimore (1995b) draws attention to SER's confirmation of the potential power of schools to affect the life chances of their students. Although the differences in scholastic attainment achieved by the same student in contrasting schools is unlikely to be great, in many instances it represents the difference between success and failure and operates as a facilitating or inhibiting factor in higher education. When coupled with the promotion of other pro-social attitudes, behaviours and positive self-image, the potential of the school to improve the life chances of students is considerable (Mortimore, 1995b, quoted in Mortimore, 1998: 143). Nonetheless SER does not suggest that schools can by themselves put right all the problems affecting students' lives. The need for schools serving disadvantaged intakes to receive extra support remains strong (Mortimore and Whitty, 1997).

There are important connections at the pupil level between academic achievement, motivation, behaviour, attendance and self-esteem. These links are often reciprocal, poor attainment increasing the risk of subsequent poor behaviour and attendance and vice versa (Rutter *et al.*, 1979; Reynolds, 1982; Mortimore *et al.*, 1988; Smyth, 1999). There are strong arguments for focusing on these links in improvement initiatives since programmes which address only one aspect in isolation (be it academic achievement, attendance, behaviour or self-esteem) are liable to have less impact in the long term. Focusing on pupils' experiences and views of school and the involvement of pupils and parents are identified as important foci of school improvement projects and initiatives designed to promote social inclusion (Riley *et al.*, 2000).

Monitoring is identified as an important tool for school improvement to help evaluate performance, set targets, assist in school development planning and provide evidence of any impact (Fitz-Gibbon, 1991, 1992, 1996; also Elliot *et al.*, 1998). The need to monitor the educational outcomes of different groups especially those from socio-economically disadvantaged and minority ethnic backgrounds and those pupils with low levels of initial attainment is relevant to improvement initiatives and promoting inclusion.

School improvement literature highlights the importance of school (and in secondary schools, departmental) culture. The impact of key individuals, often the headteacher, in the change process is also highlighted. A clear focus on a limited set of aims or targets shared by staff is also associated with more successful improvement initiatives, and increasing the school's focus on the teaching and learning process.

SER findings cannot provide 'quick fixes' for schools in difficulties (Reynolds, 1996; Stoll and Myers, 1997) and should not be treated prescriptively. They are best used to stimulate reflection and as tools to assist the development of schools as learning institutions (MacGilchrist *et al.*, 1997; Harris *et al.*, 1997). Although it is important to recognise that schools may resist pressure for change, initiatives that focus on the different components of school culture and monitor student progress seem to be more likely to have an impact. Involving pupils, teachers and parents, seeking their views and addressing their concerns should be seen as an essential part of school improvement initiatives which aim to foster inclusion (see MacBeath, 1999a; MacBeath and Mortimore, 2000). Research suggests that successful school improvement must involve the conscious commitment and involvement of teachers and managers in schools.

Education cannot remedy social exclusion on its own but remains an important means of implementing policies intended to combat social disadvantage. The social empowerment argument is a vital one, because nearly 25 years of research in the SER field suggests that the life chances of students from socio-economically disadvantaged backgrounds in particular are enhanced by effective schools – those which foster both cognitive progress and promote social and affective outcomes including motivation, self-esteem and pupil involvement.

## Notes

1 For more detailed discussions of the school effectiveness and improvement fields see: Purkey and Smith, 1983; United States Department of Education, 1986; NWREL, 1990; Firestone, 1991; Mortimore, 1991a, b, 1995a, b, 1998; Riddell and Brown, 1991; Louis and Miles, 1992; McGaw *et al.*, 1992; Scheerens, 1992; Creemers, 1994; Reynolds *et al.*, 1994; Stoll and Fink, 1994, 1996; Sammons, 1996, 1999; Goldstein, 1997, 1998; Scheerens and Bosker, 1997; Gray and Wilcox, 1995; Gray *et al.*, 1999; Townsend *et al.*, 1999; Teddlie and Reynolds, 2000; Wendel, 2000.
2 Saunders (1999) provides a detailed analysis of the development of the value added concept.
3 School 'connectedness' includes aspects such as whether pupils believe 'your teachers care about you', 'you are close to people at the school', 'you feel safe at school' and 'teachers treat students fairly'.
4 Methodological considerations in school effectiveness research have been reviewed by: Scheerens, 1992; Creemers, 1994, Goldstein, 1987, 1997, 1998; Hill and Rowe, 1996; Creemers and Reezigt, 1997.
5 For other research examining the impact of the department at the secondary

level see: Ainley, 1994; Luyten, 1994; Witziers, 1994; Harris *et al.,* 1995; and Smyth, 1999.

6  An example of an approach which blends school improvement and effectiveness methods is the *Improving the Quality of Education for All* (IQEA) project (Hopkins *et al.,* 1996).

7  The National Commission on Education's series of case studies – *Success Against the Odds* (NCE, 1996) – of successful schools in disadvantaged areas is also relevant.

8  Paterson (1998) found similar effects using different methodologies.

9  Other criticisms are included in White and Barber (1997). For detailed responses to such criticisms see Sammons *et al.* 1996; Sammons and Reynolds 1997; and Mortimore and Sammons 1997. A special issue of the international journal *School Effectiveness and School Improvement* (2001) is devoted to a consideration of twenty years of SER and focuses on analysing 'Critique and Response' with contributions from Thrupp (2001) who addresses sociological and political concerns and Slee and Weiner (2001) who examine SER in relation to educational reform and inclusive schooling. Responses to these concerns are provided by Teddlie and Reynolds 2001; Townsend 2001; and Scheerens *et al.* 2001.

# 8 Strategies and issues for inclusive schooling

*Carol Campbell, David Gillborn, Ingrid Lunt, Pamela Sammons, Carol Vincent, Simon Warren and Geoff Whitty*

This chapter synthesises strategies and key issues relating to 'inclusive schooling' based on our international review of relevant established and emerging research evidence. A clear message is that the concept of an 'inclusive school' is complex and contested. Inclusive schooling can be associated with a range of principles and purposes, with differing implications for the national, local and school-level strategies endorsed and implemented. There are tensions between a perception of an 'inclusive school' as meeting the needs of all children in a similar manner and the need to develop differential practices relating to different forms of inclusionary and exclusionary pressures, for example linked to social disadvantage or identified special educational needs.

Throughout this book, we have provided an overview of strategies which evidence suggests may be of benefit in seeking to develop 'inclusive schooling'. We have addressed a diverse range of issues. The need to bring together multi-disciplinary perspectives and researchers to consider new futures for inclusive schooling has been advocated (see Booth and Ainscow, 1998; Corbett and Slee, 2000). While there remain differences in perspectives, there are some aspects of convergence developing for inclusive schooling (see Corbett and Slee, 2000). Therefore, we have identified some key strategies and often these are common across the focus of our enquiries (for example, linked to 'special educational needs', 'race' and ethnicity, gender and social disadvantage). While inclusive schools may share features of healthy schools, child-friendly schools, improving schools and effective schools (see Chapters 1, 2, 6 and 7), in themselves these features and associated processes are not necessarily sufficient to create an 'inclusive school' where the focus must be on inclusive practices, processes and outcomes. A synthesis of the strategies that we have identified is outlined below and presented as a table in the Appendix. An exhaustive account is not possible, but the strategies and features outlined provides an indicative list of those which emerged as important from our review of the research.

It must be stressed that research relating to 'inclusive schooling' requires further development, not least because current evaluations are frequently small scale, tentative and inconclusive. Within the overall movement to 'inclusive schools', different approaches and goals have been adopted, making an overall evaluation of all strategies problematic. Localised developments may also not be applicable or replicable at a national level or even in other localities. Hence, the strategies presented below are indicative not exhaustive. The strategies are not intended as a 'quick fix' recipe for success or a 'blueprint' for all schools. Different approaches may be necessary for different schools with different needs in different local circumstances. Indeed, the need for fundamental reform at all levels of the education system to reflect diverse needs and rights has been emphasised.

## Strategies

### *Monitoring and evaluation are integral*
The development of appropriate monitoring at all levels of the education system (national, local authority, school and within school) is integral to the development and evaluation of inclusive schooling. Such monitoring must be rigorous in methodology and sensitive to the differential experiences of different groups, for example based on an analysis of 'race', gender, 'special educational needs' and socio-economic status. Raw 'league table' type measures of attainment are not adequate. Rather the monitoring of a range of processes and outcomes is required, including attendance, rates of exclusion (temporary and permanent), subject choices, attainment, staying on rates and leaver destinations. Studies of pupil progress and the 'value added' by schools are important (see Chapter 7). In developing inclusive schooling, there is a need also for systematic and careful national and local (LEA and school-level) evaluations, focusing on both processes

(for example, approaches to implementation, action plans, development plans, curriculum change, management and leadership) and outcomes (such as those indicated for monitoring). Consideration should also be given to the development of appropriate practices and processes of self-evaluation for 'inclusive schools'. However, caution needs to be exercised in attempts to measure inclusive schooling; there may be tensions between processes and outcomes associated with inclusion and those which can easily be measured based on academic attainment.

### Inclusive leadership

The importance of developing leadership (again at all levels of the education system) that promotes and embodies inclusive values and practices for schools has been clearly established. Within schools, the commitment of the headteacher to developing and embedding 'inclusive schooling' has been demonstrated to be fundamental. It has been suggested that headteachers who can be role models in challenging discrimination may be important. It is vital that headteachers for inclusive schools promote equity, oppose discrimination and seek to address disadvantage through their vision and in school policies and practices. However, such inclusive leadership cannot be the responsibility of the headteacher alone. It is necessary to encourage a shared vision of, and commitment to, inclusive schooling, which encourages the development of 'inclusive leadership' throughout the school, potentially involving all staff and pupils.

### Inclusive whole school ethos and culture

Envisioning, articulating, creating, embedding and developing a whole school ethos and culture that promotes inclusive schooling is crucial. As Corbett and Slee (2000) have indicated, developing inclusive cultures is both the most important and difficult aspect of developing inclusive schools. We would anticipate that such a culture would focus on equity issues and challenge discrimination and disadvantage. However, within these broad parameters, individual schools will develop particular 'inclusive cultures' reflecting, for example, the needs and values of their pupils and staff, institutional needs, history and approaches, and their local context, including parents and communities. It is an obvious point that some schools already have more developed 'inclusive cultures' than others. We do not suggest that developing an inclusive culture throughout all schools will be easy; however, it is fundamental to supporting inclusive policies and practices within schools.

*High expectations of all pupils*
Within an inclusive whole school ethos and culture, the promotion of high expectations of all pupils is encouraged. In short, underachievement is unacceptable for any group of pupils. The influence and impact of teacher expectations and attitudes towards pupils should be considered, for example linked to assumptions about 'special educational needs', disability, 'race', gender, socio-economic status and 'ability'. The Scottish Consultative Council on the Curriculum posed the following question for 'teaching for effective learning': 'What assumptions do I make about individual learners when I teach? On what are these assumptions based?' (SCCC, 1996: 33).

Such questions are also pertinent to 'teaching for inclusive learning'. Therefore, an awareness and development of teacher expectations for pupils appropriate to inclusive schooling is important. A focus and emphasis on pupil achievements rather than a deficit view of pupils as 'problems' or having 'problems' are vital. Furthermore, awareness of pupils' own expectations and attitudes is central to encouraging their high expectations of themselves and education.

*Valuing pupil perspectives and involvement*
Alongside high expectations for pupils is the consideration and encourage-ment of their involvement in the development of inclusive schools. As appropriate to the age of the pupil, the importance of pupil voice in school processes and decision-making has been indicated. For example, profes-sional adult interpretations of pupils' needs and wants may be very different from the real needs and wants articulated directly by pupils (see Chapter 6). Therefore, inclusive schools should consider means to involve pupil perspectives to inform the development of school-level inclusive policies and practices.

Within the UK and internationally research about children, from a range of disciplines not just education, has advocated the need to engage with children directly to understand their experiences, expectations and attitudes, rather than relying on adult and professional interpretations (Borland *et al.*, 1998; Moss *et al.*, 1999). The findings of a review – *Education and Care Away From Home* (1998) – provides insights from pupils in public care about appropriate (and inclusive) schooling:

> the key ingredients are a supportive school environment and sensitive arrangements for individual pupils. A school culture which welcomes diversity, fosters peer and staff support and does not tolerate bullying, helps children feel valued and supported and promotes the kind of trust which allows specific learning or social needs to be openly addressed. Both academic and emotional needs need to be catered for. Young people want teachers to focus primarily on their education; while being well informed of the ways in which their current circumstances may affect how they work and learn. They warn against the dangers of making assumptions or stereotyping and emphasise that each child who becomes looked after has individual needs and preferences. Consulting each pupil is thus essential.
>
> (Borland *et al.*, 1998: 110)

These pupils had clear ideas of how they expected to be treated: they wanted their individual and diverse needs recognised and addressed, but they did not want to be overtly singled out for 'different' treatment.

We are not advocating that schools should be required to undertake substantial qualitative research in order to gather information about their pupils. But rather schools should explore simple ways to involve pupils in developing inclusive schools. This should involve a commitment to listen to pupils and not to patronise them (see Gillborn, 1995).

*Clear and consistent whole school policies*
The development of clear and consistent whole school policies promoting inclusive practices is required. Building on the above strategies, such whole school policies would seek to develop equitable practices addressing processes and outcomes of disadvantage and discrimination. An

emphasis on early intervention and a preventive focus, rather than wholly reactive approaches to 'remedy' situations, should be encouraged. Such 'early intervention' and 'prevention' can take a range of forms, including for example an academic focus on the early years and pupils' learning and development, or a 'support' focus on the promotion of healthy behaviours and health advice. There should also be clear and consistent whole school policies which are strong on issues of harassment, behaviour and attendance. These policies, and linked resourcing requirements, should be integral to the school development plan.

### Promotion of inclusive learning and teaching strategies

The curriculum itself can be more or less inclusive and exclusive (see for example Chapter 3). Therefore, it is necessary to consider carefully appropriate inclusive and non-discriminatory curricula across all subject areas. For example, such curricula would emphasise anti-racist and anti-sexist approaches in all subjects. The importance of curriculum coverage for numeracy and literacy has also been indicated (see Chapter 7). Child-centred inclusive curricula and teaching methods have been widely advocated. Recently the development of a 'child-friendly' ethos and practices have been promoted (WHO, 1999). However, evidence suggests that child-centred practices may currently be more firmly embedded in primary schooling (e.g. Darling, 1999) compared to secondary schooling (e.g. Bryce and Humes, 1999a). It is also apparent that the term 'child-centred' has been used too broadly and without specification in some cases. There is a need therefore to consider the most appropriate and inclusive curricula for different age ranges and stages of schooling. In particular, the current emphasis on early years and early intervention; the need to address learning and transitions in the first and second years of secondary schooling; and the appropriate combination of academic and vocational curricula for secondary school pupils are all important in relation to inclusive schooling. The involvement and support of parents/ carers in curricula initiatives (both at home and in school) has also been advocated.

## Inclusive classroom structures and practices

It is necessary to consider the most appropriate teaching methods and classroom organisations to promote inclusionary processes and outcomes. There has been considerable debate as to whether mixed ability teaching or setting by attainment is more appropriate and effective (see for example, Boaler, 1997; Boaler *et al.* 2000; Bryce and Humes, 1999b; Gillborn and Youdell, 2000). The question for this review is which is more inclusive? In Chapter 3, we have argued that mixed ability teaching is more appropriate, as setting by attainment is neither effective nor inclusive.[1] Processes of setting and streaming institutionalise inequality and, while some pupils may improve their attainment, others will not; relative levels of attainment and disadvantage will not be adequately addressed and may even worsen.

School effectiveness and school improvement research in schools in socially disadvantaged areas identified benefits associated with structured and interactive whole class teaching (see Chapter 7). Research with pupils has advocated the combination of whole class teaching with supported individualised learning and appropriate differentiation (Kirkwood, 1999; Simpson and Ure, 1993). It is recognised that developing appropriate differentiation for all pupils across all levels of schooling will present challenges for teachers. However, significantly, research with pupils indicates their support for these practices (Simpson and Ure, 1993). Kirkwood (1999: 426) synthesises the approaches pupils expected their teachers to take:

* Identifying and responding to a range of needs;
* Building on strengths and addressing weaknesses;
* Promoting the belief that attainment can improve (by the teacher demonstrating that by applying certain agreed procedures pupils can become good learners and achieve something);
* Identifying targets and criteria for success;
* Setting realistically high expectations which pupils can achieve, with support;
* Giving feedback on attainments and problems (praise and encourage-

ment are important but pupils also want to know where they are performing badly and how to put it right);

- Using a self-referenced rather than norm- or criterion-referenced approach to enable pupils to see how they are progressing;
- Employing a range of sources of support, including older pupils, parents, learning support teachers and library staff;
- Sharing the management of learning (but pupils must also be given the information and support to cope effectively with responsibilities).

The need to develop inclusive approaches to assessment have also been recognised. Research has indicated the need to develop formative approaches, which make assessment part of the dialogue about progress and target-setting, and to investigate means of actively involving pupils in such processes (see for example, Simpson, 1999).

## *Additional supports for pupils and staff*
The provision of a range of 'support' for pupils and staff, as necessary and appropriate, has been endorsed. The precise nature of such support will vary depending on the school, pupils and staff. However, in developing inclusive schooling, the need for a combination of academic support, pastoral support and (as appropriate) health and social supports have been indicated. The extension of school hours, for example, to include study support activities has been promoted. Teaching staff may require support in developing and implementing inclusive learning and teaching strategies (as indicated above), ranging from a supportive school culture, structure and management; support in classrooms, for example through 'classroom assistants', EAL assistants and for learning support; and support in their professional development. This is clearly an area where material, as well as staff resources, are of critical importance.

## *Recognition and respect for community languages*
We have indicated the importance of appropriate strategies for recognising community languages in classrooms, across the school and in communications with parents and the wider community. The development of EAL

approaches within classrooms (rather than pupils being removed from classrooms or placed in specific groupings within class) and throughout the school is important for this strategy (see Chapters 3 and 5).

*Inclusive staff collaboration and teamwork*
The importance of staff collaboration and teamwork, at the levels of the classroom, department and whole school, are import to enabling inclusive practices and processes and in facilitating professional development. In developing school-linked inter-agency strategies, staff collaboration and the development of appropriate and effective teams is a crucial, but frequently difficult, process (see Chapter 6). A key issue is the need for clear role relationships among the different professionals required to work together. This can be facilitated by attention to the structure of working relationships and the organisation of integrated services, plus the development of a collaborative culture.

*Positive action to promote good social relationships*
The development of positive and appropriate relationships throughout the school, including interactions among staff, between staff and pupils, and among pupils, is important to the development of (socially) inclusive schools. The encouragement and development of pupils' inter-personal skills are recognised as vital to a pupil's educational, emotional, mental and social development. School policies and teachers' practices should recognise and promote what is regarded as positive pupil behaviour. Within the curriculum, the inclusion of personal, social and health education and sex and relationships education requires attention (see for example, Chapter 4).

*Inclusive communication*
In developing a shared vision of inclusive schooling, creating related policies and encouraging appropriate practices, attention is required to the modes and purposes of communication throughout the school, including staff and pupils. Attention needs to be given to the most relevant and useful forms of communication with parents, communities and other

agencies (see Chapter 5). This will involve consideration of the languages to be used also (see above).

### Inclusive parental and family involvement

Developing inclusive practices requires schools to consider means to encourage appropriate home–school links (see Chapter 5). Such a strategy requires the development of two-way communication between school staff and parents/carers, rather than one-way information given by the school to parents. Consideration of approaches that will encourage the active engagement of parents/carers and families in schools and education is central to developing these relationships. In such a process, it is necessary to recognise that schools may benefit from a range of support from parents/carers, for example in directly educational activities or in governance roles. Schools may also be able to offer considerable support to parents and families, for example in the provision of adult education or in the provision of health, childcare and social supports.

### Inclusive inter-school collaboration

Benefits of schools collaborating together to create socially and educationally inclusive practices have been noted also. For example, in Chapter 2, the development of school clusters to support SEN provision is discussed. Attention to collaboration and links between primary and secondary schools has been highlighted in easing the transfer and transition of pupils between these stages of schooling. Recent initiatives, such as New Community Schools in Scotland and Education Action Zones in England, highlight also the potential for schools to co-operate in order to tackle aspects of social disadvantage, social inclusion and educational underachievement (see Sammons *et al.*, 2000).

### Inclusive inter-agency collaboration

New Community Schools in Scotland and Education Action Zones in England exemplify also initiatives to develop inter-agency collaborations (public, private and third sectors) to promote more inclusive approaches to schooling (see for example, Power *et al.*, 2001). Health promoting and

healthy schools indicate the importance of involving health-related promotion and activities in meeting pupils' health needs. The further extension of health and social supports, for example as evident in USA full
service schools, have been suggested to encourage a holistic approach to
pupils' educational, physical, emotional, mental and social development.
We have suggested that such processes are vital to inclusive schooling
when they attempt to tackle barriers to learning and to offer supports that
will help to facilitate educational (and other) development and learning
(see Chapter 6).

### Inclusive community involvement

It has been argued that in addressing social inclusion and social disadvantage, schools should also review their relationships with local communities. The school can be viewed as community resource, for example
a physical meeting place which may provide community facilities, such
as access to a library, IT facilities and adult education. Therefore, the
school can offer support to local communities. On the other hand, local
communities may also offer support to the school, for example in recent
initiatives in mentoring schemes. However, while aspects of encouraging
community engagement in inclusive schooling have been advocated,
identifying processes for doing this requires further investigation. There
is considerable debate as to what constitutes a school's community or
indeed its potentially multiple communities with differing requirements.

### Provision of adequate financial and other resources

Developing and maintaining inclusive schools requires attention to and
investment of resources. While not all strategies require substantial
financial investment, adequate planning and provision of time and
resources are important. Where initiatives do require financial investment, consideration needs to be given to initial costs and the need for
ongoing funding. For example, in developing extended school services in
the USA, the need for stable and long-term funding has been highlighted
(see Chapter 6). Issues of sustainability need to be considered as early as
possible. The most important resource is appropriate and adequate

staffing and the need for their professional development (see the following section).

*Continuing professional development*
The importance of appropriate and relevant professional development for all staff involved in inclusive schools has been stressed. Such professional development should involve a range of training and other opportunities. There are some activities that are relevant to all staff involved, such as consideration of the principles, processes and outcomes of inclusive schooling. There is also clearly a need for specific development opportunities depending on the roles of individuals and groups of staff. In moving towards inter-agency collaborations, there is a need for the provision of joint multi-disciplinary and inter-agency training to aid understanding and working practices between the individuals involved. In the longer term, it may be necessary to consider related reforms in initial teacher education (and other appropriate professionals' training) to incorporate issues of inclusive schooling.

## Issues for future development

The strategies we have identified are derived from research across different aspects of inclusive schooling, linked to 'special educational needs', 'race', gender, social disadvantage, parental involvement, inter-agency working and school effectiveness and school improvement research. While noting some differences in perspectives, we have developed a synthesis of evidence relating to good practice. The strategies we have synthesised are relevant to the wider development of inclusive schooling.

However, original empirical research with schools that exhibit all or most of these strategies was beyond the remit of this review. It is important to note that further research in this area is required; for example, we have indicated that some of the research is based on small-scale and localised initiatives and/or is inconclusive at the present time. There is a need for research also into the processes and outcomes associated with different strategies proposed for inclusive schooling in different combinations for different schools and contexts. In short, are all the strategies compatible in all cases? Are certain strategies consistently essential? Does the importance of some strategies vary depending on specific factors? Are certain combinations mutually reinforcing or in tension? What we do know, however, is that schools can be more or less inclusive and that schools can reinforce or amplify wider processes of discrimination and disadvantage; we know also that schools can develop strategies based on a concern to promote equity and to challenge disadvantage and discrimination.

Although we have presented general strategies, it is important to recognise that universal and uniform reforms alone may not be appropriate. There are important and necessary strategies for all schools, for example non-discriminatory curricula and teaching methods and an inclusive culture, but there is also a need to recognise differences between and within schools. While schools require support in developing 'inclusive' policies and practices, there is a need also for local flexibility and school-level decision-making about the most appropriate goals to meet particular school and pupil needs, albeit within a potentially national framework. The balance between the importance of local initiatives and flexibility, with the need for a national framework and policies, requires further investigation.

The principle of creating inclusive schools to benefit all pupils is widely endorsed; however there are concerns that an all-encompassing definition of inclusion may fail to differentiate the specific and multiple needs of individuals and groups of students. There needs to be a recognition that a focus on equality of opportunity will not necessarily generate equality of outcome (see Pantazis, 2000). Evidence suggests that universal reform strategies may create what appear to be overall improvements, while leaving existing processes of discrimination and disadvantage largely intact. Therefore, there is a need to consider carefully the overall development of 'inclusive schooling' for all, alongside the need for specific interventions and supports to tackle particular forms of exclusion, disadvantage and underachievement. Monitoring of the experiences, processes and outcomes of schools for all students and specific students is vital.

However, monitoring is not an end in itself, but rather part of a wider process that developing inclusive schooling requires changes in schools. In such a process, the perceptions and experiences of pupils, parents/carers and teachers could be central to further research and policy development.

Within schools, it is apparent that inclusive approaches are multi-dimensional involving whole school policies, departmental practices, classroom approaches and the expectations, attitudes and perspectives of teachers and pupils. There is a need for ongoing research concerning these processes and practices. However, current research suggests that inequalities associated with class, 'race' and gender are often reinforced and amplified through the operation of these processes (Gillborn and Youdell, 2000). Inclusive schooling is set in a context of exclusive processes internal and external to schools.

It is necessary to recognise that schools moving towards becoming more 'inclusive' will be at different stages of development and are not 'empty vessels' (Rivers *et al.*, 1999: 23). Rather, existing good practices need to be recognised, valued and developed. However, this recognition needs to be balanced with the evidence that achieving change through incremental 'add ons' may not result in as thorough reform as may be required to implement and embed developed inclusive schools. These have been argued to require reconsideration of the purpose, structures, processes and outcomes of schooling. Realistically though, initiatives that can be integrated with and help to develop existing practices and priorities are most likely to succeed.

In developing inclusive schools, it is also necessary to consider processes and outcomes both within and beyond schools, for example, relating to health, citizenship, parental involvement and community development. Both removing the *barriers* to learning and developing strategies which *enable* learning must be central to 'inclusive schooling'. While this book is concerned with schools specifically, the development of genuinely inclusive practices requires wider social, economic and political changes.

## Concluding remarks

Conceptually, the term 'inclusive schooling' has been broadened from a focus mainly on 'special educational needs' to the 'needs' of all pupils, and further to include their parents/carers, families and local communities. The development of (socially and educationally) inclusive schools has been widely supported, particularly alongside commitments to social inclusion and social justice. However, as we have indicated, careful consideration of the multiple and diverse needs of individuals and groups of students are required. There is a concern also if the notion of 'inclusive schooling for all' becomes perceived as a 'one size fits all' approach; in which a discourse of need, diversity and recognition is combined with a practice of assimilation and essentially an ongoing 'deficit' view of those who do not appear to 'fit in'. It is important to recognise that there are differences in educational experiences and outcomes not only between different groups of pupils, but also within groups, requiring monitoring and research of the differential educational outcomes for individuals and groups of pupils.

Writing about schooling and the influence of social class, ethnicity and gender, McBride proposed:

> the achievement of an education system fully committed to both equality and to quality will not be easy, in more than one sense of the word 'easy'. It is not easy to conceptualise such a system when all education systems perpetuate, although to different extents, inequalities in the wider society in which they exist. It is not easy in that the practical steps needed will be difficult to achieve, requiring vision and labour ... the difficulties inherent in the process are no reason for abandoning it but rather a reason for approaching the process with more determined care and knowledge.
>
> (McBride, 1992: iv)

Such issues are pertinent to the development of inclusive schooling. The purpose of our review has been to synthesise and develop existing knowledge and research. Furthermore, as Brown and Riddell suggested, there has been 'a need to shift the emphasis from the documentation of failure to an analysis of the conditions which lead to good practice' (1992: 176). Our review has focused on issues and strategies relevant to principles, policies and practices associated with inclusive schooling.

We would argue that inclusive schools are concerned with recognising and addressing disadvantage and discrimination for all pupils. Inclusive schooling must take seriously the important task of appreciating diversity and addressing discrimination and disadvantage in schooling and for pupils, linked to debates about equity and justice. To promote inclusionary processes and outcomes and reduce exclusionary ones, inclusive education is an important development, which must be considered alongside wider social and economic policies, for example tackling child poverty and reducing social disadvantage and discrimination. The development of 'inclusive schools' is a large, complex and, at times, controversial task. However, it is clear that 'including' pupils and creating equality cannot be simply perceived as providing children with access to school. It requires consideration of inclusive and equitable processes and outcomes throughout 'inclusive education'. Such developments are important, necessary and overdue.

# Note

1 As we noted in Chapter 3, evidence suggests that such internal selection does not lead to any *net* improvement in results.

# References

ACE (Advisory Centre for Education) (1996) *An Evaluation of the LEAP Project.* London: ACE.

Aggleton, P. (1987) *Rebels Without a Cause?* Lewes: Falmer.

Aggleton, P., Rivers, K., Mulvihill, C., Chase, E., Downie, A., Sinkler, P., Tyrer, P. and Warwick, I. (2000) 'Lessons learned: working towards the National Healthy School Standard'. *Health Education* 100(3): 102–10.

Ainley, J. (1994) 'Curriculum areas in secondary schools: differences in student response'. Paper presented at the International Congress for School Effectiveness and School Improvement, Melbourne, Australia.

Ainley, P. (1993) *Class and Skill: Changing divisions of knowledge and labour.* London: Cassell.

Ainscow, M. (1995) 'Education for all: making it happen'. Keynote Address, International Special Education Congress, Birmingham, July 1995.

—— (1997) 'Towards inclusive schooling'. *British Journal of Special Education* 24(1): 3–6.

—— (1998) 'Exploring links between special needs and school improvement'. *Support for Learning* 13: 70–6.

—— (1999) *Understanding the Development of Inclusive Schools.* London: Falmer.

Ainscow, M., Farrell, P., Tweddle, D. and Malki, G. (1999) 'The role of LEAs in developing inclusive policies and practices'. *British Journal of Special Education* 26(3): 136–40.

Alladina, S. (1995) *Being Bilingual: A guide for parents, teachers and young people on mother tongue, heritage language and bilingual education.* Stoke-on-Trent, Trentham.

Allen, J. (1999) *Actively Seeking Inclusion. Pupils with special needs in mainstream schools.* London: Falmer.

Amin, K., Drew, D., Fosam, B. and Gillborn, D. with Demack, S. (1997) *Black and Ethnic Minority Young People and Educational Disadvantage.* London: Runnymede Trust.

Apple, M.W. (1999) 'How the conservative restoration is justified', in M.W. Apple, *Power, Meaning and Identity: Essays in critical educational studies.* New York: Peter Lang.

Armstong, D., Armstrong, F. and Barton, L. (2000) 'Introduction: what is this book about?', in F. Armstrong, D. Armstrong and L. Barton (eds) *Inclusive Education: Policy, contexts and comparative perspectives.* London: David Fulton.

Arnot, M., David, M. and Weiner, G. (1996) *Educational Reform and Gender Equality in Schools* (Research Discussion Series no. 17). London: Equal Opportunities Commission.

Arnot, M., Gray, J., Rudduck, J. and Duveen, G. (1998) *Recent Research on Gender and Educational Performance* (Ofsted Reviews of Research). London: The Stationary Office.

Arnot, M., Weiner, G. and David, M. (1999) *The Gender Gap*. Cambridge: Polity.

Arrowsmith, J. (1990) *Improving Home–School Communication in the Secondary School* (Spotlight, no. 30). Edinburgh: Scottish Council for Research in Education (SCRE).

Arshad, R. and Almeida Diniz, F. (1999) 'Race equality in Scottish education', in T.G.K. Bruce and W.M. Humes (eds) *Scottish Education*. Edinburgh: Edinburgh University Press.

ALAOME (Association of LEA Advisory Officers for Multicultural Education) (2000) *Guidance on Target-setting to Raise Minority Ethnic Achievement*. Oxford: ALAOME.

Audit Commission/HMI (1992) *Getting in on the Act. Provision for pupils with special educational needs: the national picture*. London: HMSO.

Australian Centre for Equity Through Education (1998) *Thinking About Full Service Schools No.3: Working Together: Integrated school-linked services in Saskatchewan*. Sydney: ACEE.

Back, L. (1996) *New Ethnicities and Urban Culture: Racisms and multiculture in young lives*. London: UCL Press.

Ballard, K. (ed.) (1999) *Inclusive Education: International voices on disability and justice*. London: Falmer Press.

Banks, J.A. (1994) *Multiethnic Education: Theory and practice*, 3rd edn. Boston: Allyn and Bacon.

—— (1997) *Educating Citizens in a Multicultural Society*. New York: Teachers College Press.

Barber, M. (1999) 'Taking the tide at the flood: transforming the middle years'. Paper presented at the Middle Years of Schooling Conference, Melbourne Australia, 28 March.

Barber, M. and Dann, R. (eds) (1996) *Raising Educational Standards in the Inner Cities: Practical initiatives in action*. London: Cassell.

Barclay, P. (1995) *Income and Wealth, Volume 1: Report of the Inquiry Group*. York: Joseph Rowntree Foundation.

Barton, L. (1997) 'Inclusive education: romantic, subversive or realistic?' *International Journal of Inclusive Education* 1(3): 231–42.

Bastiani, J. (1996) *Home–School Contracts and Agreements – Opportunity or threat?* London: Royal Society of Arts.

Battistich, V. and Hom, H. (1997) 'The relationship between students' sense of their school as a community and their involvement in problem behaviours'. *American Journal of Public Health* 87(12): 1197–2001.

Benn, C. and Chitty, C. (1997) *Thirty Years On: Is comprehensive education alive and well or struggling to survive?* London: Penguin Books.

Bernstein, B. (1970) 'Education cannot compensate for society'. *New Society* 387: 344–7.

Bhatti, G. (1999) *Asian Children at Home and at School: An ethnographic study.* London: Routledge.

Blair, A. and Waddington, M. (1997) 'The home–school "contract": regulating the role of parents'. *Education and the Law* 9(4): 291–305.

Blair, M. (1998) 'The myth of neutrality in educational research', in P. Connolly and B. Troyna (eds) *Researching Racism in Education: Politics, theory and practice.* Buckingham: Open University Press: 12–20.

Blair, M. and Bourne, J. with Coffin, C., Creese, A. and Kenner, C. (1998) *Making the Difference: Teaching and learning strategies in successful multi-ethnic schools.* London: DfEE.

Blair, M., Gillborn, D., Kemp, S. and MacDonald, J. (1999) 'Institutional racism, education and the Stephen Lawrence Inquiry'. *Education and Social Justice* 1(3): 6–15.

Blyth, E. and Milner, J. (1993) 'Exclusion from school: a first step in exclusion from society?' *Children and Society* 7(3): 255–68.

Boaler, J. (1997) *Experiencing School Mathematics.* Buckingham: Open University Press.

Boaler, J., William, D. and Brown, M. (2000), 'Students' experience of ability grouping – disaffection, polarisation and the construction of failure'. *British Educational Research Journal* 26: 631–48.

Booth, T. (1996) 'Changing views of research on integration: the inclusion of students with "special needs" or participation for all?', in A. Sigston, P. Curran, A. Labram and S. Wolfendale (eds) *Psychology in Practice with Young People, Families and Schools.* London: David Fulton.

—— (2000) 'Inclusion and exclusion policy in England: who controls the agenda?', in F. Armstrong, D. Armstrong and L. Barton (eds) *Inclusive Education: Policy, contexts and comparative perspectives.* London: David Fulton.

Booth, T. and Ainscow, M. (1998) *From Them To Us: An international study of inclusion in education.* London: Routledge.

Booth, T., Ainscow, M., Black-Hawkins, K., Vaughan, M. and Shaw, L. (2000) *Index for Inclusion: Developing learning and participation in schools.* Bristol: Centre for Studies on Inclusive Education (CSIE).

Booth, T., Ainscow, M. and Dyson, A. (1997) 'Understanding inclusion and exclusion in the English competitive education system'. *International Journal of Inclusive Education* 1(4): 337–56.

Borland, M., Pearson, C., Hill, M., Tisdall, K. and Bloomfield, I. (1998) *Education and Care Away from Home.* Edinburgh: Scottish Council for Research in Education (SCRE).

Borthwick-Duffy, S.A., Palmer, D.S. and Lane, K.L. (1996) 'One size doesn't fit all: full inclusion and individual differences'. *Journal of Behavioral Education* 6: 311–29.

Boscardin, M.L. and Jacobson, S. (1996) 'The inclusive school: integrating diversity and solidarity through community-based management'. *Journal of Educational Administration* 35(5): 466–76.

Bosker, R. (1995) 'De stabiliteit van Mattheus-effecten'. Paper presented at the Annual Conference of the Dutch Educational Research Association (Onderwijs-researchdagen), Groningen, June.

Bosker, R. J. and Scheerens, J. (1994) 'Alternative models of school effectiveness put to the test', in R.J. Bosker, B.P.M. Creemers and J. Scheerens (eds) *Conceptual and Methodological Advances in Educational Effective Research: Special issue of the International Journal of Educational Research*, 21(2): 159–80.

Boyd, W.L., Crowson, R.L. and Gresson, A. (1997) *Neighbourhood Initiatives, Community Agencies, and the Public Schools: A changing scene for the development and learning of children* (Publication Series no.6). Mid-Atlantic Laboratory for Student Success, Temple University, USA, www.temple.edu/LSS/L97-6.htm.

Brah, A. and Minhas, R. (1985) 'Structural racism or cultural difference: schooling for Asian girls', in G. Weiner (ed.) *Just a Bunch of Girls: Feminist approaches to schooling.* Milton Keynes: Open University Press.

Brandt, G.L. (1986) *The Realization of Anti-Racist Teaching.* Lewes: Falmer.

Briar-Lawson, K., Lawson, H.A., Collier, C. and Joseph, A. (1997) 'School-linked comprehensive services: promising beginnings, lessons learned, and future challenges'. *Social Work in Education* 19: 136–48.

Brooks, R., Sukhnandan, L., Flanagan, N. and Sharp, C. (1999) *Creating a Climate for Learning: Strategies to raise achievement at Key Stage 2.* Slough: NFER.

Brown, A. (1993) 'Participation, dialogue and the reproduction of social inequalities', in R. Mertens and J. Vass (eds) *Partnership in Maths.* London: Falmer.

Brown, P. and Lauder, H. (1992) 'Education, economy and society: an introduction to a new agenda', in P. Brown and H. Lauder (eds) *Education for Economic Survival.* London: Routledge.

Brown, P. and Lauder, H. (1996) 'Education, globalisation and economic development'. *Journal of Education Policy* 11(1): 1–25.

Brown, S. and Riddell, S. (1992) 'Equality in education – old dilemmas and new possibilities', in S. Brown and S. Riddell (eds) *Class, Race and Gender in Schools: A new agenda for policy and practice in Scottish education.* Edinburgh: Scottish Council for Research in Education (SCRE).

Brown, S., Riddell, S. and Duffield, J. (1996) 'Possibilities and problems of small scale studies to unpack the findings of large scale studies of school effectiveness', in J. Gray, D. Reynolds, C. Fitz-Gibbon and D. Jesson (eds) *Merging Traditions: The future of research on school effectiveness and school improvement.* London: Cassell.

Bruner Foundation (1993) *Community Schools: The Bruner Foundation's evaluation of the New York Community Schools Program.* New York: Bruner Foundation Inc.

Bryce, T. and Humes, W. (1999a) 'Scottish secondary education: philosophy and practice', in T. Bryce and W. Humes (eds) *Scottish Education.* Edinburgh: Edinburgh University Press.

Bryce, T. and Humes, W. (eds) (1999b) *Scottish Education.* Edinburgh: Edinburgh University Press.

Bryk, A. and Raudenbush, S. (1992) *Hierarchical Linear Models.* New York: Sage.

Burchardt, T., Le Grand, J. and Piachaud, D. (1999) 'Social exclusion in Britain 1991–1995'. *Social Policy and Administration* 33(3): 227–44.

Capper, L. (2000) 'Share – a national parental involvement programme', in S. Wolfendale and J. Bastiani (eds) *The Contributions of Parents to School Effectiveness.* London: David Fulton.

Carlberg, C. and Kavale, K. (1980) 'The efficacy of special versus regular class placement for exceptional children'. *Journal of Special Education* 14: 295–309.

Carlson, C. (1996) 'Changing the school culture toward integrated services'. *Special Services in the Schools* 11(1/2): 225–49.

Carrim, N. (1996) 'Working with and through difference in antiracist pedagogies'. *Journal of International Studies in Sociology of Education* 1: 25–38.

Carrim, N. and Soudien, C. (1999) 'Critical antiracism in South Africa', in S. May, *Critical Multiculturalism: Rethinking multicultural and antiracist education.* London: Falmer.

Chamberlayne, P. (1997) 'Social exclusion: sociological traditions and national contexts', in Sostris (ed.) *Social Exclusion in Comparative Perspective: Social strategies in risk societies* (Sostris Working Paper 1). London: University of East London, Centre for Biography in Social Policy.

Chaskin, R.J. and Richman, H.A. (1993) 'Concerns about school-linked services: institution-based versus community-based models'. *Education and Urban society* 25(2): 201–11.

Clark, C., Dyson, A. and Millward, A. (1995) 'Towards inclusive schools: mapping the field', in C. Clark, A. Dyson and A. Millward (eds) *Towards Inclusive Schools?* London: David Fulton: 164–78.

Clough, P. (ed.) (1998) *Managing Inclusive Education. From policy to experience.* London: Paul Chapman.

Clough, P. and Corbett, J. (2000) *Theories of Inclusive Education: A students' guide.* London: Paul Chapman.

Cole, M. (ed.) (2000) *Education, Equality and Human Rights: Issues of gender, 'race', sexuality, special needs and social class.* London: Routledge/Falmer.

Coleman, J., Campbell, C., Hobson, E., McPartland, J., Mood, A., Weinfeld, F. and York, R. (1966) *Equality of Educational Opportunity.* Washington: National Center for Educational Statistics/US Government Printing Office.

Connell, R.W. (1996a) *Masculinities,* Cambridge: Polity.

—— (1996b) 'Teaching the boys: new research on masculinity, and gender strategies for schools'. *Teachers College Record* 98(2).

Connolly, P. (1998) *Racism, Gender Identities and Young Children: Social relations in a multi-ethnic, inner-city primary school.* London: Routledge.

Corbett, J. (1999) 'Inclusivity and school culture: the case of special education', in J. Prosser (ed.) *School Culture.* London: Paul Chapman.

Corbett, J. and Slee, R. (2000) 'An international conversation on inclusive education', in F. Armstrong, D. Armstrong and L. Barton (eds) *Inclusive Education: Policy, contexts and comparative perspectives.* London: David Fulton.

Cousins, C. (1998) 'Social exclusion in Europe: paradigms of social disadvantage in Germany, Spain, Sweden and the United Kingdom'. *Policy and Politics* 26(2): 127–46.

Creemers, B. (1994) *The Effective Classroom.* London: Cassell.

Creemers, B. and Reezigt, G. (1997) 'School effectiveness and school improvement: sustaining links'. *School Effectiveness and School Improvement* 8(4): 396–429.

Crockett, J.B. and Kauffman, J.M. (1999) *The Least Restrictive Environment: Its origins and interpretations in special education.* Mahwah, New Jersey: Lawrence Erlbaum.

Croll, P. and Moses, D. (2000a) 'Ideologies and utopias: education professionals' views of inclusion'. *European Journal of Special Needs Education* 15(1): 1–12.

Croll, P. and Moses, D. (2000b) 'Resources, policies and educational practice', in B. Norwich (ed.) *Developments in Additional Resource Allocation to Promote Greater Inclusion.* Stafford: NASEN.

Crowson, R.L. and Boyd, W.L. (1996a) 'Structures and strategies: toward an understanding of alternative models for coordinated children's services', in J.G. Cibulka and W.J. Kritek (eds) *Coordination Among Schools, Families and Communities.* Albany: State University of New York Press.

Crowson, R.L. and Boyd, W.L. (1996b) 'Achieving coordinated school-linked services: facilitating utilization of the emerging knowledge base'. *Educational Policy* 10(2): 253–72.

Crowson, R.L. and Boyd, W.L. (1999) *New Roles for Community Services in Educational Reform* (Publication Series no.5). Mid-Atlantic Laboratory for Student Success, Temple University, USA, www.temple.edu/LSS/99-5.pdf.

Crowther, D., Dyson, A. and Millward, A. (1998) *Costs and Outcomes for Pupils with Moderate Learning Difficulties in Special and Mainstream Schools.* London: DfEE.

Crozier, G. (1998) 'Parents and schools: partnership and surveillance'. *Journal of Education Policy* 13(1): 125–36.

CSIE (1989) *The Integration Charter.* Bristol: Centre for Studies in Inclusive Education (CSIE).

—— (1996) *Developing an Inclusive Policy for Your School.* Bristol: Centre for Studies in Inclusive Education (CSIE).

—— (2000) *Index for Inclusion.* Bristol: Centre for Studies in Inclusive Education (CSIE).

Cuckle, P. (1997) 'The school placement of pupils with Down's syndrome in England and Wales'. *British Journal of Special Education* 24: 175–80.

Cunningham, C., Glenn, S., Lorenz S., Cuckle, P. and Shepperdson, B. (1998) 'Trends and outcomes in educational placements for children with Down's syndrome'. *European Journal of Special Needs Education* 13: 225–37.

Dadzie, S. (2000) *Toolkit for Tackling Racism in Schools.* Stoke-on-Trent: Trentham.

Danby, J. and Cullen, C. (1988) 'Integration and mainstreaming: a review of the efficacy of mainstreaming and integration for mentally handicapped pupils'. *Educational Psychology* 8: 177–95.

Daniels, H. and Garner, P. (1999) *Inclusive Education. World Yearbook of Education 1999.* London: Kogan Page.

Darling, J. (1999) 'Scottish primary education: philosophy and practice', in T. Bryce and W. Humes (eds) *Scottish Education.* Edinburgh: Edinburgh University Press.

David, M. (1993) *Parents, Gender and Education Reform.* Cambridge: Polity Press.

David, M., Edwards, R., Hughes, M. and Ribbens, J. (1993) *Mothers and Education: Inside out?* London: Macmillan.

Davies, B. (1989) *Frogs and Snails and Feminist Tales: Pre-school children and gender.* Sydney: Allen and Unwin.

—— (1993) *Shards of Glass: Children reading and writing beyond gendered identities.* St Leonards: Allen and Unwin.

Debnath, E. (1998) 'Youth, gender and community change: a case study of young Bangladeshis in Tower Hamlets'. Unpublished PhD thesis, University of Cambridge.

Deem, R., Brehony, K. and Heath, S. (1995) *Active Citizenship and the Governing of Schools*. Buckingham: Open University Press.

Demack, S., Drew, D. and Grimsley, M. (2000) 'Minding the gap: ethnic, gender and social class differences in attainment at 16 (1988–95)'. *Race Ethnicity and Education* 3(2): 117–43.

DES (Department of Education and Science) (1978) *Special Educational Needs. The Warnock Report*. London: HMSO.

DeWitt Wallace-Reader's Digest Fund (1999) *An Overview of the Extended-Service Schools Initiative*. New York: DeWitt Wallace-Reader's Digest Fund.

DfE (Department for Education) (1994) *Code of Practice on the Identification and Assessment of Special Educational Needs*. London: HMSO.

DfEE (Department for Education and Employment) (1997a) 'Excellence for all children: meeting special educational needs'. Government Green Paper. London: DfEE.

—— (1997b) *Excellence in Schools*. London: DfEE.

—— (1998a) *Meeting Special Educational Needs. A programme of action*. London: DfEE.

—— (1998b) *Meeting the Childcare Challenge*. London: HMSO. http://www.dfee.gov.uk/childcare/content3.htm

—— (1999) *National Healthy School Standard Guidance*. London: HMSO.

—— (2000a) *Schools Plus*. London: HMSO.

—— (2000b) *Sure Start*. London: HMSO. http://www.surestart.gov.uk/text/aboutWhatIs.cfm

Douglas, N. and Kemp, S. with Aggleton, P. and Warwick, I. (2000) *Sexuality Education in Four Local Secondary Schools: Learning from a local initiative*. London: EHH Gay Men's Project/London Borough of Hounslow.

Douglas, N., Warwick, I., Kemp, S. and Whitty, G. (1997) *Playing it Safe: Responses of secondary school teachers to lesbian, gay and bisexual pupils, bullying, HIV and AIDS education and Section 28*. London: Health and Education Research Unit, Institute of Education, University of London.

Drew, D. (1995) *'Race', Education and Work: The statistics of inequality*. Aldershot: Avebury.

Driscoll, M.E., Boyd, W.L. and Crowson, R.L. (1998) *Collaborative Services Initiatives: A report of a national survey of programs* (Publication Series no.3). Mid-Atlantic Laboratory for Student Success, Temple University, USA, www.temple.edu/LSS/pub98-3.htm.

Dryfoos, J.G. (1995), 'Full service schools: revolution or fad?' *Journal of Research on Adolescence* 5: 147–72.

Dyson, A. and Gains, C. (1993) 'Special needs and effective learning: towards a collaborative model for the year 2000', in A. Dyson and C. Gains (eds) *Rethinking Special Needs in Mainstream Schools Towards the Year 2000*. London: David Fulton.

Dyson, A. and Robson, E. (1999) *School Inclusion: The evidence. A review of the literature on school–family–community links*. York: Joseph Rowntree Foundation/ National Youth Agency.

Earley, P., Fidler, B. and Ouston, J. (eds) (1996) *Improvement Through Inspection? Complementary approaches to school development*. London: David Fulton.

Eber, L., Nelson, C. and Miles, P. (1997) 'School-based Wrap-around for students with emotional and behavioral difficulties'. *Exceptional Children* 63(4): 539–55.

Edmonds, R.R. (1979) 'Effective schools for the urban poor'. *Educational Leadership* 37(1): 15–27.

Edwards, V. (1986) *Language in a Black Community*. London: Multilingual Matters.

Elliot, K., Smees, R. and Thomas, S. (1998) 'Making the most of your data: school self-evaluation using value added measures'. *Improving Schools* 1(3).

Elliott, J. (1996) 'School effectiveness research and its critics: alternative visions of schooling'. *Cambridge Journal of Education* 26(2): 199–223.

Epstein, D. (ed.) (1994) *Challenging Lesbian and Gay Inequalities in School*. Buckingham: Open University Press.

Epstein, D. and Johnson, R. (1998) *Schooling Sexualities*. Buckingham: Open University Press.

Epstein, J. (1996) 'Perspectives and previews on research and policy for school, family and community partnerships', in A. Booth and J. Dunn (eds) *Family–School Links: How do they affect educational outcomes?* Mahwah, NJ: Lawrence Erlbaum.

European Commission (1995) *Teaching and learning – towards the learning society*. White Paper. Brussels, Office for Official Publications of the European Communities.

Eurostat (1997) Reported in *The Guardian*, 28 April.

Evans, J. and Lunt, I. (1994) *Markets, Competition and Vulnerability: Some effects of recent legislation on children with special needs*. London: Institute of Education, University of London.

Evans, J., Lunt, I., Wedell, K., and Dyson, A. (1999) *Collaborating for Effectiveness*. Buckingham: Open University Press.

Farrell, P. (1997) 'The integration of children with severe learning difficulties: a review of the recent literature'. *Journal of Applied Research in Learning Disabilities* 10: 1–14.

Farrell, P. (2000) 'The impact of research on developments in inclusive education'. *International Journal of Inclusive Education* 4(2):153–62.

—— (2001) 'Special education in the last twenty years: have things really got better?' *British Journal of Special Education* 28(1): 3–9.

Farrell, P. and Mittler, P. (1998) *Policy and Practice in the Assessment of Pupils with Special Educational Needs*. Manchester: Rathbone.

Feiler, A. and Gibson, H. (1999) 'Threats to the inclusive movement'. *British Journal of Special Education* 26(3): 147–52.

Fielding, S., Daniels, H., Creese, V., Hey, V. and Leonard, D. (1999) 'The (mis)use of SATs to examine gender and achievement at Key Stage 2'. *The Curriculum Journal* 10(2): 169–87.

Figueroa, P. (1991) *Education and the Social Construction of 'Race'*. London: Routledge.

— (1995) 'Multicultural education in the United Kingdom: historical development and current status', in J.A. Banks and C.A. McGee-Banks (eds) *Handbook of Research on Multicultural Education*. New York: Simon and Schuster Macmillan.

Firestone, W.A. (1991). 'Introduction', in J.R. Bliss, W.A. Firestone and C.E. Richards (eds) *Rethinking Effective Schools: Research and practice*. Englewood Cliffs, NJ: Prentice Hall.

First, P.F., Curcio, J.L. and Young, D.L. (1993) 'State full-service school initiatives: new notions of policy development'. *Politics of Education Association Yearbook, 1993*: 63–73.

Fish, J. and Evans, J. (1995) *Managing Special Education: Codes, charters and competition*. Buckingham: Open University Press.

Fitz-Gibbon, C.T. (1991) 'Multilevel modelling in an indicator system', in S.W. Raudenbush and J.D. Willms (eds) *Schools, Classrooms and Pupils International Studies of Schooling from a Multilevel Perspective*. San Diego: Academic Press.

—— (1992). ' School effects at A level: genesis of an information system', in D. Reynolds and P. Cuttance (eds) *School Effectiveness Research, Policy and Practice*. London: Cassell.

—— (1996) *Monitoring Education Indicator: Quality and effectiveness*. London: Cassell.

Flising, B. (1995) Samverkan skola-skolbarnsomsorg, SoS-rapport 1995: 12 (Cooperation school – school-age child care, SoS-report 1995: 12). Stockholm: Socialstyrelen (National Board of Health and Social Welfare).

Florian, L. (1998) 'An examination of the practical problems associated with the implementation of inclusive education policies'. *Support for Learning* 13(3): 105–8.

Francis, B. (1998) *Power Plays: Primary school children's constructions of gender, power and adult work*. Stoke-on-Trent: Trentham Books.

—— (2000) *Boys, Girls and Achievement: Addressing the classroom issues*. London: Routledge/Falmer.

French, J. and French, P. (1993) 'Gender imbalances in the primary classroom: an interactional account', in P. Woods and M. Hammersley (eds) *Gender and Ethnicity in Schools: Ethnographic accounts*. London: Routledge.

Frith, R. and Mahony, P. (eds) (1994) *Promoting Quality and Equality in Schools: Empowering teachers through change*. London: David Fulton.

Fuchs, D. and Fuchs, L.S. (1994) 'Inclusive schools movement and the radicalisation of special education reform'. *Exceptional Children* 60: 294–309.

Fullan, M. (1991) *The New Meaning of Educational Change*. London: Cassell.

—— (1993) *Change Forces: Probing the depths of educational reform*. London: Falmer.

Gallie, W.B. (1956) 'Essentially contested concepts'. *Proceedings of the Aristotelian Society* 56: 167–98.

Gardner, S. (1993) 'Afterword'. *Politics of Education Association Yearbook, 1993*: 189–99.

Gartner, A. and Lipsky, D. (1987) 'Beyond special education: toward a quality system for all students'. *Harvard Educational Review* 57(4): 367–95.

Garvin, J.R. and Young, A.H. (1993) 'Resource issues: a case study from New Orleans'. *Politics of Education Association Yearbook, 1993*: 93–106.

Gewirtz, S. (1998) 'Conceptualizing social justice in education: mapping the territory'. *Journal of Education Policy* 13(4): 469–84.

Gewirtz, S., Ball, S. and Bowe, R. (1995) *Markets, Choice and Equity*. Buckingham: Open University Press.

Giangreco, M. F. (1997) 'Key lessons learned about inclusive education: summary of the 1996 Schonell Memorial Lecture'. *International Journal of Disability, Development and Education* 44(3): 193–206.

Giangreco, M.F., Dennis, R., Cloninger, C., Edelman, S. and Schattman, R. (1993) '"I've counted Jon": transformational experiences of teachers educating students with disabilities'. *Exceptional Children* 59: 359–72.

Gillborn, D. (1990) *'Race', Ethnicity and Education: Teaching and learning in multi-ethnic schools*. London: Unwin Hyman.

—— (1995) *Racism and Antiracism in Real Schools: Theory, policy, practice*. Buckingham: Open University Press.

—— (1998a) 'Racism and the politics of qualitative research: learning from controversy and critique', in P. Connolly and B. Troyna (eds) *Researching Racism in Education: Politics, theory and practice*. Buckingham: Open University Press: 34–54.

—— (1998b) 'Race and ethnicity in compulsory schooling', in T. Modood and T.

Acland (eds) *Race and Higher Education: Experiences, challenges and policy implications*. London: Policy Studies Institute: 11–23.

—— (2000) 'Anti-racism: from policy to praxis', in B. Moon, S. Brown and M. Ben-Peretz (eds) *Routledge International Companion to Education*. London: Routledge: 476–88.

Gillborn, D. and Gipps, C. (1996) *Recent Research on the Achievements of Ethnic Minority Pupils*. Report for the Office for Standards in Education. London: HMSO.

Gillborn, D. and Mirza, H.S. (2000) *Educational Inequality: Mapping race, class and gender. A synthesis of research evidence for the Office for Standards in Education*. London: Ofsted.

Gillborn, D. and Youdell, D. (2000) *Rationing Education: Policy, practice, reform and equity*. Buckingham: Open University Press.

Goldstein, H. (1987). *Multilevel Models in Educational and Social Research*. London: Charles Griffin.

—— (1997) 'Methods in school effectiveness research'. *School Effectiveness and School Improvement* 8(4): 369–95.

—— (1998) *Models for Reality: New approaches to the understanding of educational processes*. London: Institute of Education, University of London.

Goldstein, H., Rashbash, J., Yang, M., Woodhouse, G., Pan, H., Nuttall, D. and Thomas, S. (1993) 'A multilevel analysis of school examination results'. *Oxford Review of Education* 19(4): 425–33.

Gomby, D.S. and Larson, C.S. (1992) 'Evaluation of school-linked services'. *Future of Children* 2(1): 68–84.

Goodman, A., Johnson, P. and Webb, S. (1997) *Inequality in the UK*. Oxford: Oxford University Press.

Granovetter, M. (1973) 'The strength of weak ties'. *American Journal of Sociology of Education* 78: 1360–80.

Grant, C. (1989) 'Equity, equality, teachers and classroom life', in W. Secada (ed.) *Equity in Education*. Philadelphia: Falmer.

Gray, J. (1990) 'The quality of schooling: frameworks for judgements'. *British Journal of Educational Studies* 38(3): 204–33.

—— (1998) *The Contribution of Educational Research to the Cause of School Improvement: A professorial lecture*. London: Institute of Education, University of London.

—— (2000) *Causing Concern But Improving: A review of schools' experiences* (DfEE Research Brief no. 188, June). London: DfEE.

Gray, J., Goldstein, H. and Jeson, D. (1996) 'Changes and improvements in schools' effectiveness: trends over five years'. *Research Papers in Education* 11(1): 35–51.

Gray, J., Hopkins, D., Reynolds, D. and Wilcox, B. (1999) *Improving Schools: Performance and potential.* Buckingham: Open University Press.

Gray, J. and Wilcox, B. (1995) 'The challenge of turning round ineffective schools', in J. Gray and B. Wilcox (eds) *Good School, Bad School.* Buckingham: Open University Press.

Gray, P. and Dessent, T. (1993) 'Getting our act together'. *British Journal of Special Education* 20(1): 9–11.

Green, P. (1999) *Raise the Standard: A practical guide to raising ethnic minority and bilingual pupils' achievement informed by policy and practice in cities across the European Community.* Stoke-on-Trent: Trentham.

Hallam, S. and Toutounji, I. (1996) *What Do We Know About the Grouping of Pupils by Ability? A Research Review.* London: Institute of Education, University of London.

Hallgarten, J. (2000) *Creating Stakeholder Schools.* London: IPPR.

Halpern, D. (1999) *Social Capital: The new golden goose?* London: Nexus/IPPR.

Halsey, A.H., Heath, A.F. and Ridge, J.M. (1980) *Origins and Destinations: Family, class, and education in modern Britain.* Oxford: Clarendon Press.

Hamilton, D. (1996) 'Peddling feel-good fictions', *Forum* 38(2): 54–6.

Hamilton, K. and Saunders, L. (1997) *The Health Promoting School: A summary of the ENHPS evaluation project in England.* London: Health Education Authority.

Hargreaves, D. (1995) 'School effectiveness, school change and school improvement: the relevance of the concept of culture'. *School Effectiveness and School Improvement* 6(1): 23–46.

Harris, A., Bennett, N. and Preedy, M. (eds) (1997) *Organizational Effectiveness and Improvement in Education.* Buckingham: Open University Press.

Harris, A., Jamieson, I. and Russ, J. (1995) 'A study of effective departments in secondary schools'. *School Organisation* 15(3): 283–99.

Hatcher, R. (1997) 'New Labour, school improvement and racial inequality'. *Multicultural Teaching* 15(3): 8–13.

—— (1998) 'Social justice and the politics of school improvement and effectiveness'. *Race, Ethnicity and Education* 1(2): 267–89.

Hay McBer (2000) *Research into Teacher Effectiveness: A model of teacher effectiveness.* Report by Hay McBer to the DfEE, June. London: DfEE.

Hayton, A. (1999) 'Boys and girls underachieving: issues for 14+ education and training', in A. Hayton (ed.) *Tackling Disaffection and Social Exclusion.* London: Kogan Page: 156–77.

Hazekamp, J.L. and Popple, K. (eds) (1997) *Racism in Europe: A challenge for youth policy and youth work.* London: UCL Press.

Hegarty, S. (1993) 'Reviewing the literature on integration'. *European Journal of Special Needs Education* 8(3): 194–200.

—— (1998) 'Challenges to inclusive education: a European perspective', in S.J. Vitello and A. Mithaug (eds) *Inclusive schooling: National and international perspectives*. Mahwah, NJ: Lawrence Erlbaum.

Heward, C. (1988) *Making a Man of Him: Parents and their sons' education at an English public school 1929–1950*. London: Routledge.

Hill, P. and Rowe, K. (1996) 'Multilevel modelling in school effectiveness research'. *School Effectiveness and School Improvement* (7)1: 1–34.

Hill, P. and Rowe, K. (1998) 'Modelling student progress in studies of educational effectiveness'. *School Effectiveness and School Improvement* 9(3): 310–33.

Hillman, J. and Stoll, L. (1994) *Understanding School Improvement* (SIN Research Matters no. 1). London: International School Effectiveness and Improvement Centre, Institute of Education, University of London.

Hills, J. (1995) *Income and Wealth, Volume 2: A summary of evidence*. York: Joseph Rowntree Foundation.

—— (1998) *Income and Wealth: The latest evidence*. York: Joseph Rowntree Foundation.

Hobbs, B.B. (1994) 'Collaboration between schools and community agencies in rural settings'. *ERS Spectrum* (summer): 25–33.

Hofman, R.H. (1999) 'The contribution of clusters to integration'. *European Journal of Special Needs Education*-14(3): 187–97.

Honig, M.I. and Jehl, J.D. (1999) 'Toward a Federal support system for connecting educational improvement strategies and collaborative services'. Paper presented at the Improving Results for Children and Families by Connecting Collaborative Services with School Reform Efforts, Washington, 26–7 January.

Hopkins, D. (1994) 'School improvement in an era of change', in P. Ribbens and E. Burridge (eds) *Improving Education Promoting Quality in Schools*. London: Cassell.

Hopkins, D., Ainscow, M. and West, M. (1996) *School Improvement in an Era of Change*. London: Cassell.

Hornby, G. (1992) 'Integration of children with special educational needs: is it time for a policy review?' *Support for Learning* 7(3): 130–4.

—— (1999) 'Inclusion or delusion: can one size fit all?' *Support for Learning* 14(4): 152–7.

Horsch, K. (1998), *Evaluating School-Linked Services: Considerations and best practices*. Cambridge, MA: Harvard Family Research Project.

Hughes, D. and Lauder, H. (1999) *Trading in Futures: Why markets in education don't work*. Buckingham: Open University.

Hunt, P. and Goetz, L. (1997) 'Research in inclusive educational programs, practices and outcomes for students with severe learning disabilities'. *The Journal of Special Education* 31(1): 3–29.

Jackson, D. and Salisbury, J. (1996) 'Why should secondary schools take boys seriously?' *Gender and Education* 8(1): 103–15.

Jeffcoate, R. (1984) *Ethnic Minorities and Education.* London: Harper and Row.

Jencks, C., Smith, M., Acland, H., Bane, M.J., Cohen, D., Gintis, H., Heyns, B. and Michelson, S. (1972). *Inequality: A reassessment of the effects of family and schooling in America.* New York: Basic Books.

Jenkinson, J. (1997) *Mainstream or Special? Educating students with disabilities.* London: Routledge.

Jensen, J. (1989) 'The talent of women, the skills of men: flexible specialisation and women', in S. Wood (ed.) *The Transformation of Work.* London: Unwin Hyman.

Jones, C. and Rutter, J. (1998) *Refugee Education: Mapping the field.* Stoke-on-Trent: Trentham.

Jordan, L. and Goodey, C. (1996) *Human Rights and School Change: The Newham story.* Bristol: Centre for Studies on Inclusive Education (CSIE).

Jowett, S., Baginsky, M. and MacNeil, M. (1991) *Building Bridges: Parental involvement in school.* Windsor: NFER-Nelson.

Joyce, B., Calhoun, E. and Hopkins, D. (1999) *The New Structure of School Improvement Inquiring Schools and Achieving Students.* Buckingham: Open University Press.

Joyce, B. and Showers, B. (1988) *Student Achievement Through Staff Development.* New York: Longman.

Kadel, S. and Routh, D. (1993) 'Implementing collaborative services: new challenges for practitioners and experts in reform'. *Politics of Education Association Yearbook, 1993*: 121–34.

Kauffman, J.M. (1995) 'The regular education initiative as Reagan–Bush education policy: a trickle down theory of education of the hard-to-teach', in J.M. Kauffman and D.P. Hallahan (eds) *The Illusion of Full Inclusion: A comprehensive critique of a current special education bandwagon.* Austin: PRO-ED.

Kauffman, J.M. and Hallahan, D.P. (eds) (1995) *The Illusion of Full Inclusion: A comprehensive critique of a current special education bandwagon.* Austin: PRO-ED.

Kehily, M.J. and Nayak, A. (1997) '"Lads and laughter": humour and the production of heterosexual hierarchies'. *Gender and Education* 9(1): 69–88.

Kenway, J. and Willis, S., with Blackmore, J. and Rennie, L. (1998) *Answering Back: Girls, boys and feminism in schools.* London: Routledge.

Kinchloe, J. and Steinberg, S. (1997) *Changing Multiculturalism.* Philadelphia: Open University Press.

Kirkwood, M. (1999) 'Classroom management in the secondary school', in Bryce, T. and Humes, W. (eds) *Scottish Education.* Edinburgh: Edinburgh University Press.

Kirst, M.W. (1994) 'Equity for children: linking education and children's services'. *Educational Policy* 8: 583–90.

Klein, G. (1993) *Education Towards Race Equality.* London: Cassell.

Kritek, W.J. (1996) 'Introduction', in J.G. Cibulka and W.J. Kritek (eds) *Coordination Among Schools, Families, and Communities: Prospects for educational reform.* Albany: State University of New York Press: ix–xxv.

Kumar, K. (1992) 'New theories of industrial society', in P. Brown and H. Lauder (eds) *Education for Economic Survival.* London: Routledge.

Lane, T.S. (1998) 'School-linked services in action: results of an implementation project'. *Social Work in Education* 20(1): 37–47.

Larabee, D. (1999) 'No exit: public education as a public good'. Paper presented to the 50th Anniversary Event of The Japan Society of Educational Sociology, Tokyo, August.

Lee, V., Bryk, A., and Smith, J. (1993) 'The organisation of effective secondary schools', in L. Darling-Hammond (ed.) *Research in Education* 19: 171–226, Washington: American Educational Research Association.

Leithwood, K. and Louis, K.S. (1999) *Organizational Learning in Schools.* Lisse: Swets and Zeitlinger.

Leney, T. (1999) 'European approaches to social exclusion' in A. Hayton (ed.) *Tackling Disaffection and Social Exclusion.* London: Kogan Page.

Levine, D. and Lezotte, L. (1990) *Unusually Effective Schools: A review and analysis of research and practice.* Madison, WI: National Center for Effective Schools Research and Development.

Lewis, A. and Norwich, B. (2000) *Mapping a Pedagogy for Special Educational Needs.* Exeter and Warwick: University of Exeter and University of Warwick.

Lindsay, G. (1997) 'Are we ready for inclusion?', in G. Lindsay and D. Thompson (eds) *Values into Practice in Special Education.* London: Fulton.

Lipietz, A. (1992) *Towards a New Economic Order.* Cambridge: Polity.

Lipsky, D.K. and Gartner, A. (1996) 'Inclusion, school restructuring and the remaking of American society'. *Harvard Educational Review* 66(4): 762–95.

Lipsky, D.K. and Gartner, A. (1998) 'Taking inclusion into the future'. *Educational Leadership* 58: 78–81.

Lloyd, C. (2000) 'Excellence for all children – false promises! The failure of current policy for inclusive education and implications for schooling in the 21st century'. *International Journal of Inclusive Education* 4(2): 133–51.

London Borough of Tower Hamlets (1997) *Analysis of 1996 GCSE Results by Pupil Background Factors*. London: London Borough of Tower Hamlets.

Louis, K.S. and Miles, M. (1991) 'Toward effective urban high schools: the importance of planning and coping', in J.R. Bliss, W.A. Firestone and C.E. Richards (eds) *Rethinking Effective Schools: Research and practice*. Englewood Cliffs, NJ: Prentice Hall.

Louis, K.S. and Miles, M. (1992) *Improving the Urban High School: What works and why*. London: Cassell.

Low, C. (1997) 'Is inclusivism possible?'. *European Journal of Special Needs Education* 12(1): 71–9.

Lunt, I. and Evans, J. (1994) *Allocating Resources for Special Educational Needs*. Stafford: NASEN.

Lunt, I., Evans, J., Norwich, B. and Wedell, K. (1994) *Working Together: Interschool collaboration for special needs*. London: David Fulton.

Lunt, I. and Norwich, B. (1999) *Can Effective Schools Be Inclusive Schools?* London: Institute of Education, University of London.

Luyten, H. (1994) 'Stability of school effects in secondary education: the impact of variance across subjects and years'. Paper presented at the annual meeting of the American Educational Research Association, New Orleans, 4–8 April.

—— (1995) 'Teacher change and instability across grades'. *School Effectiveness and School Improvement* 1(1): 67–89.

Lynch, J. (1986) *Multicultural Education: Principles and practice*. London: Routledge and Kegan Paul.

Mac an Ghaill, M. (1988) *Young, Gifted and Black: Student–teacher relations in the schooling of Black youth*. Milton Keynes: Open University Press.

—— (1989) 'Coming-of-age in 1980s England: reconceptualising Black students' schooling experience'. *British Journal of Sociology of Education* 10(3): 273–86.

—— (1994) *The Making of Men: Masculinities, sexualities and schooling*. Buckingham: Open University Press.

—— (1999) *Contemporary Racisms and Ethnicities: Social and cultural transformations*. Buckingham: Open University Press.

MacBeath, J. (1999a) *Schools Must Speak for Themselves: The case for school self-evaluation*. London: Routledge.

—— (1999b) 'School effectiveness and school improvement', in T.G. Bruce and W.M. Humes (eds) *Scottish Education*. Edinburgh: Edinburgh University Press.

MacBeath, J. and Mortimore, P. (eds) (2000) *Improving School Effectiveness*. Buckingham: Open University Press.

McBride, G. (1992) 'Preface: Realising Rhetoric', in S. Brown and S. Riddell (eds)

*Class, Race and Gender in Schools.* Edinburgh: Scottish Council for Research in Education (SCRE).

McCarthy, C. and Crichlow, W. (1993) 'Theories of identity, theories of representation, theories of race', in C. McCarthy and W. Crichlow (eds) *Race, Identity and Representation in Education.* New York: Routledge: xiii–xxix.

McClure, M. and Lindle, J. (eds) (1997) *Expertise versus Responsiveness in Children's Worlds.* London: Falmer.

McDonnell, J. (1987) 'The integration of students with severe handicaps into regular public schools: an analysis of parents' perceptions of potential outcomes'. *Education and Training in Mental Retardation* 22: 98–111.

McGaw, B., Piper, K., Banks, D. and Evans, D. (1992) *Making Schools More Effective: Report of the Australian Effective Schools Project.* Victoria: Australian Council for Educational Research.

MacGilchrist, B., Myers, R. and Reed, J. (1997) *The Intelligent School.* London: Paul Chapman.

McGlynn, A. and Stalker, H. (1995) 'Recent developments in the Scottish process of school inspection'. *Cambridge Journal of Education* 25(1): 13–22.

McLaren, P. (1995) *Critical Pedagogy and Predatory Culture.* New York: Routledge.

McPherson, A. (1992) *Measuring Value Added in Schools* (National Commission on Education Briefing no. 1). London: National Commission on Education.

Macpherson, W. (1999) *The Stephen Lawrence Inquiry.* CM 4262-I. London: The Stationery Office.

Madaus, G., Kellingham, T., Rakow, E., and King, D. (1979) 'The sensitivity of measures of school effectiveness'. *Harvard Educational Review* 49: 207–30.

Madden, N.A. and Slavin, R.F. (1983) 'Mainstreaming students with mild handicaps: academic and social outcomes'. *Review of Educational Research* 53: 519–89.

Majors, R., Gillborn, D. and Sewell, T. (1998) 'The exclusion of Black children: implications for a racialized perspective'. *Multicultural Teaching* 16(3): 35–7.

Manset, G. and Semmel, M.I. (1997) 'Are inclusive programs for students with mild disabilities effective? A comparative review of model programs'. *Journal of Special Education* 31: 155–80.

Market Street Research (1997) *Impact of School-Linked Services on Families and Children: Follow-up outcome assessment 1997/1998.* Northampton, MA: Market Street Research.

—— (1998) *Outcomes of Massachusetts School-Linked Service Initiative for Participating Schools, Agencies, and Businesses.* Northampton, MA: Market Street Research.

Martin, J., Ranson, S. and Rutherford, D. (1995) 'The annual parents' meeting: potential for partnership'. *Research Papers in Education* 10(1): 19–49.

Martin, J. and Vincent, C. (1999) 'Parental voice: an exploration'. *International Studies in Sociology of Education* 9(3): 231–52.

Mason, D. (2000) *Race and Ethnicity in Modern Britain*, 2nd edn. Oxford: Oxford University Press.

Matthews, P. and Smith, G. (1995) 'Ofsted: inspecting schools and improvement through inspection'. *Cambridge Journal of Education* 25(1): 23–34.

May, S. (1999) *Critical Multiculturalism: Rethinking multicultural and antiracist education.* London: Falmer.

Meijer, C. (2000) 'Funding and inclusion', in B. Norwich (ed.) *Developments in Additional Resource Allocation to Promote Greater Inclusion.* Stafford: NASEN.

Meijer, C., Pijl, S.J. and Hegarty, S. (1994) *New Perspectives in Special Education: A six-country study of integration.* London: Routledge.

Melaville, A.I. and Blank, M.J. (1999) 'Trends and lessons in school–community initiatives'. Paper presented at the Improving Results for Children and Families by Connecting Collaborative Services with School Reform Efforts, Washington, 26–7 January.

Melnick, S.L. (2000) 'Multiculturalism: one view from the United States of America', in B. Moon, M. Ben-Peretz and S. Brown (eds) *Routledge International Companion to Education.* New York: Routledge: 456–75.

Merttens, R. and Vass, J. (1993) *Partnership in Maths.* London: Falmer.

Miller, D. (1976) *Social Justice.* Oxford: Clarendon Press.

Minami, M. and Ovando, C.J. (1997) 'Language issues in multicultural contexts', in J.A. Banks and C.A. McGee-Banks (eds) *Handbook of Research on Multicultural Education.* New York: Simon and Schuster Macmillan.

Ming, T.W. and Cheong, C.Y. (1995) 'School environment and student performance: a multilevel analysis'. Paper presented at the International Congress of School Effectiveness and Improvement, Leeuwarden, The Netherlands: January.

Mirza, H.S. (1992) *Young, Female and Black.* London: Routledge.

Mitchell, D.R. (1996) 'The rules keep changing: special education in a reforming education system'. *International Journal of Disability, Development and Education* 45(2): 55–74.

Mittler, P. (2000) *Working Towards Inclusive Education: Social contexts.* London: David Fulton.

Modood, T., Beishon, S. and Virdee, S. (1994) *Changing Ethnic Identities.* London: Policy Studies Institute.

Modood, T., Berthoud, R., Lakey, J., Nazroo, J., Smith, P., Virdee, S. and Beishon, S. (1997) *Ethnic Minorities in Britain: Diversity and disadvantage.* London: Policy Studies Institute.

Moodley, K.A. (1995) 'Multicultural education in Canada: historical development and current status', in J.A. Banks and C.A. McGee-Banks (eds) *Handbook of Research on Multicultural Education*. New York: Simon and Schuster Macmillan.

Moore, J. (1999) 'Developing a local authority response to inclusion'. *Support for Learning* 14(4): 174–8.

—— (2000) 'Developments in additional resource allocation to promote greater inclusion', in B. Norwich (ed.) *Developments in Additional Resource Allocation to Promote Greater Inclusion*. Stafford: NASEN.

Mortimore, P. (1991a) 'The nature and findings of school effectiveness research in the primary sector', in S. Riddell and S. Brown (eds) *School Effectiveness Research: Its messages for school improvement*. London: HMSO.

—— (1991b) 'Effective schools from a British perspective', in J.R. Bliss, W.A. Firestone and C.E. Richards (eds) *Rethinking Effective Schools: Research and practice*. Englewood Cliffs, NJ: Prentice Hall.

—— (1995a) *Effective Schools: Current impact and future possibilities* (The Director's Inaugural Lecture, 7 February). London: Institute of Education, University of London.

—— (1995b) 'The positive effects of schooling', in M. Rutter (ed.) *Psychological Social Disturbances in Young People: Challenges for prevention*. Cambridge: Cambridge University Press.

—— (1998) *The Road to Improvement: Reflections on school effectiveness*. Lisse: Swets and Zeitlinger.

Mortimore, P. and Sammons, P. (1997) 'Endpiece: a welcome and a riposte to critics, etc.', in J. White and M. Barber (eds) *Perspectives on School Effectiveness and Improvement* (Bedford Way Papers). London: Institute of Education, University of London.

Mortimore, P., Sammons, P., Stoll, L., Lewis, D. and Ecob, R. (1988) *School Matters: The junior years*. Wells: Open Books.

Mortimore, P., Sammons, P. and Thomas, S. (1994) 'School effectiveness and value added measures'. *Assessment in Education: Principles, Policy and Practice* 1(3): 315–32.

Mortimore, P. and Stone, C. (1990) 'Measuring educational quality', *British Journal of Educational Studies* 39(1): 69–82.

Mortimore, P. and Whitty, G. (1997) *Can School Improvement Overcome the Effects of Disadvantage?* London: Institute of Education, University of London.

Mortimore, P. and Whitty, G. (1999) 'School improvement: a remedy for social exclusion?' in A. Hayton (ed.) *Tackling Disaffection and Social Exclusion: Education perspectives and policies*. London: Kogan Page.

Moss, P. (1999) 'Going critical: childhood, parenthood and the labour market', in

S. Wolfendale and H. Einzig (eds) *Parenting Education and Support*. London: David Fulton.

Moss, P., Petrie, P. and Poland, G. (1999) *Rethinking School: Some international perspectives*. Leicester: Youth Works Press.

Muijs, R.D. and Reynolds, D. (2000) 'School effectiveness and teacher effectiveness in mathematics: some preliminary findings from the evaluation of the Mathematics Enhancement Programme (Primary)', *School Effectiveness and School Improvement* 11(3): 273–303.

Mullard, C. (1982) 'Multiracial education in Britain: from assimilation to cultural pluralism', in J. Tierney (ed.) *Race, Migration and Schooling*. London: Holt, Rinehart and Winston: 120–33.

—— (1984) *Anti-Racist Education: The three O's*. Cardiff: National Anti-racist Movement in Education.

Murphy, P. and Elwood, J. (1998) 'Gendered learning outside and inside school: influences on achievement', in D. Epstein, J. Elwood, V. Hey and J. Maw (eds) *Failing Boys? Issues in gender and achievement*. Buckingham: Open University Press.

NCE (National Commission on Education) (1996) *Success Against the Odds: Effective schooling in disadvantaged areas*. London: Routledge.

Norwich, B. (1990) 'Decision-making about special educational needs', in P. Evans and V. Varma (eds) *Special Education: Past, present and future*. Lewes: Falmer.

—— (1996) 'Special needs education or education for all: connective specialisation and ideological impurity'. *British Journal of Special Education* 23(2): 100–4.

—— (1997) *A Trend Towards Inclusion: Statistics on special school placements and pupils with statements in ordinary schools England 1992–96*. Bristol: Centre for Studies in Inclusive Education (CSIE).

—— (1999) 'The connotation of special education labels for professionals in the field'. *British Journal of Special Education* 26 (4): 179–84.

—— (2000) 'The withdrawal of inclusion 1996–98: a continuing trend by the Centre for Studies in Inclusive Education (CSIE)'. *British Journal of Special Education* 27(1): 39–40.

Nuttall, D. (1990) *Differences in Examination Performance* (RS 1277/90). London: Research and Statistics Branch, ILEA.

Nuttall, D., Goldstein, H., Prosser, R. and Rasbash, J. (1989) 'Differential school effectiveness'. *International Journal of Educational Research* 13: 769–76.

NWREL (Northwest Regional Educational Laboratory) (1990) *Onward to Excellence: Effective schooling practices: a research synthesis*. Portland, OR: Northwest Regional Educational Laboratory.

Oakes, J. (1990) *Multiplying Inequalities: The effects of race, social class, and tracking on opportunities to learn mathematics and science.* Santa Monica: The Rand Corporation.

Oakes, J. and Lipton, M. (1999) *Teaching to Change the World.* San Francisco: McGraw-Hill.

O'Brien, T. (2001) (ed.) *Enabling Inclusion: Blue skies ... dark clouds?* London: The Stationery Office.

OECD (1989) *Schools and Quality: An International Report.* Paris: OECD.

—— (1995) *Integrating Students with Special Needs into Mainstream Schools.* Paris: OECD.

—— (1997) *Parents as Partners in Schooling.* Paris: OECD.

Ofsted (Office for Standards in Education) (1999) *Raising the Attainment of Minority Ethnic Pupils.* London: Ofsted.

Ofsted (Office for Standards in Education) and EOC (Equal Opportunities Commission) (1996) *The Gender Divide: Performance differences between boys and girls at school.* London: HMSO.

Oliver, M. (1996) *Understanding Disability: From theory to practice.* Basingstoke: Macmillan.

ONS (Office for National Statistics) (1998) *Population Trends 91.* London: ONS.

Osler, A. (1997) *Exclusion from School and Racial Equality.* London: Commission for Racial Equality.

Ouston, J. (1999) 'School effectiveness and school improvement: critique of a movement', in T. Bush, L. Bell, R. Bolam, R. Glatter and P. Ribbins (eds) *Educational Management: Redefining theory, policy and practice.* London: Paul Chapman.

Pantazis, C. (2000) 'Introduction', in C. Pantazis and D. Gordon (eds) *Tackling Inequalities: Where are we now and what can be done?* Bristol: The Policy Press.

Parsons, C. (1999) *Education, Exclusion and Citizenship.* London: Routledge.

Parsons, C. and Howlett, K. (1996) 'Permanent exclusions from school: a case where society is failing its children'. *Support for Learning* 11(3): 109–12.

Paterson, L. (1998) 'Multi-variate, multi-level regression: an illustration concerning school teachers' perceptions of their pupils'. *Educational Research and Evaluation* 4(2): 126–42.

Pathak, S. (2000) *Race Research for the Future: Ethnicity in education, training and the labour market* (DfEE Research Topics Paper RTP01). London: DfEE.

Percy-Smith, J. (ed.) (2000) *Policy Responses to Social Exclusion: Towards inclusion?* Buckingham: Open University Press.

Pijl, S. and Meijer, C. (1991) 'Does integration count for much? An analysis of the practices of integration in eight countries'. *European Journal of Special Needs Education* 6(2): 100–11.

Pijl, S.J., Meijer, C. and Hegarty, S. (1997) *Inclusive Education: A global agenda.* London: Routledge.

Plewis, I. (1998) 'Curriculum coverage and classroom grouping as explanations of between teacher differences in pupils' mathematics progress'. *Educational Research and Evaluation* 4(2): 97–107.

Power, S., Campbell, C., Sammons, P., Robertson, P., Elliot, K. and Whitty, G. (2001) 'New community schools in Scotland: strategies for inclusive schooling'. Paper presented to the European Conference for Educational Research, Lille, September.

Power, S. and Clark, A. (2000) 'The right to know: parents, schools and parents' evenings'. *Research Papers in Education* 15(1): 25–48.

Power, S., Warren, S., Gillborn, D., Thomas, S. and Coate, K. (2000) *Mainstream Public Services in Deprived and Non-deprived Areas: Evidence on the quality of delivery, performance and impact* (A Report to the Social Exclusion Unit). London: Institute of Education, University of London.

Power, S., Whitty, G., Edwards, T. and Wigfall, V. (1998) 'Schoolboys and school-work: gender identification and academic achievement'. *International Journal of Inclusive Education* 2(2): 135–53.

Power, S., Whitty, G., Edwards, T. and Wigfall, V. (1999) 'Destined for success? Educational biographies of academically able youngsters'. *Research Papers in Education* 14(3): 321–39.

Powney, J. (1996) *Gender and Attainment: A review.* Edinburgh: Scottish Council for Research in Education [SCRE].

Powney, J., McPake, J., Hall, S. and Lyall, L. (1998) *Education of Minority Ethnic Groups in Scotland: A review of research.* Edinburgh: Scottish Council for Research in Education [SCRE].

Purkey, S.C. and Smith, M.S. (1983) 'Effective schools, a review'. *Elementary School Journal* 83(4): 427–52.

Putnam, R. (1995) 'Tuning in, tuning out: the strange disappearance of social capital in America'. *Political Science and Politics* 28: 1–20.

Qvarsell, B., Dovelius, J. and Eriksson, A. (1996) *Att forska och lara I narsamhallet Nya laromonster – nya arenor?* FOLK-projecktet rapport nr 1 *(Researching and learning in the local community: New educational patterns – new scenes of action? FOLK* project report no.1). Stockholm: Pedagogiska institutionen Stockholms Universitet (Department of Education, University of Stockholm).

Rawls, J. (1972) *A Theory of Justice.* Oxford: Clarendon Press.

Reay, D. (1998) *Class Work: Mothers' involvement in their children's primary schooling.* London: UCL Press.

Reid, K., Hopkins, D. and Holly, P. (1987) *Towards the Effective School.* Oxford: Blackwell.

Resnick, M.D. *et al.* (1997) 'Protecting adolescents from harm: findings from the National Longitudinal Study on Adolescent Health'. *Journal of the American Medical Association* 278: 823–32.

Reynolds, D. (1982) 'The search for effective schools'. *School Organisation* 2(3): 215–37.

—— (1995) 'The effective school: an inaugural lecture'. *Evaluation and Research in Education* 9(2): 57–73.

—— (1996) 'Turning round ineffective schools: some evidence and some speculation', in J. Gray, D. Reynolds, C. Fitz-Gibbon and D. Jesson (eds) *Merging Traditions: The future of research and school effectiveness and school improvement*. London: Cassell.

—— (1997) 'School effectiveness: retrospect and prospect (the 1997 SERA lecture)'. *Scottish Educational Review* 29(2): 97–113.

Reynolds, D., Creemers, B., Nesselrodt, P.S., Schaffer, E.C., Stringfield, S. and Teddlie, C. (1994) *Advances in School Effectiveness Research and Practice*. Oxford: Pergamon.

Reynolds, M.C., Wang, M.C. and Walberg, H.J. (1987) 'The necessary restructuring of special and regular education'. *Exceptional Children* 53: 391–8.

Richardson, R. and Wood, A. (1999) *Inclusive Schools, Inclusive Society: Race and Identity on the Agenda*. Stoke-on-Trent, Trentham.

Ribbens, J. (1994) *Mothers and their Children*. London: Sage.

Riddell, S. (1999) 'Gender and Scottish education', in T.G.K. Bryce and W.M. Humes (eds) *Scottish Education*. Edinburgh: Edinburgh University Press.

—— (2000) 'Inclusion and choice: mutually exclusive principles in special educational needs?', in F. Armstrong, D. Armstrong and L. Barton (eds) *Inclusive Education: Policy, contexts and comparative perspectives*. London: David Fulton.

Riddell, S. and Brown, S. (1991) *School Effectiveness Research : Its messages for school improvement*. Edinburgh: HMSO.

Riddell, S., Brown, S. and Duffield, J. (1994) 'Parental power and special educational needs: the case of specific learning difficulties'. *British Educational Research Journal* 20: 327–44.

Riley, K., Letch, R. and Rowles, D. (2000) *Bringing Disenfranchised Young People Back into the Frame* (Project Overview Report 1: July). London: University of Roehampton.

RISE (Research into State Education) (2000) *Home–School Agreements: A true partnership?* London: RISE.

Rivers, K., Aggleton, P., Chaise, E., Downie, A., Mulvihill, C., Sinkler, P., Tyrer, P. and Warwick, I. (1999) *Learning Lessons: A report on two research studies informing The National Healthy School Standard (NHSS)*. London: Institute of Education Thomas Coram Research Unit/Department of Health/DfEE.

Rizvi, F. and Lingard, B. (1996) 'Disability, education and the discourses of justice', in C. Christensen and F. Rizvi (eds) *Disability and the Dilemmas of Education and Justice*. Milton Keynes: Open University Press.

Roaf, C. (1988) 'The concept of a whole school approach to special needs', in O. Robinson and G. Thomas (eds) *Tackling Learning Difficulties*. London: Hodder and Stoughton.

Roaf, C. and Bines, H. (1989) *Needs, Rights and Opportunities*. Lewes: Falmer.

Robertson, P. and Toal, D. (2000) 'ISEP case studies: extending the quality framework', in J. MacBeath and P. Mortimore (eds) *Improving School Effectiveness*. Buckingham: Open University Press.

Ross, S., Smith, L. and Casey, J. (1999) '"Bridging the gap": the effects of the success for all program on elementary school reading achievement as a function of student ethnicity and ability levels'. *School Effectiveness and School Improvement* 10(2): 129–50.

Rouse, M. and Florian, L. (1996) 'Effective inclusive schools: a study in two countries'. *Cambridge Journal of Education* 26(1): 71–85.

Rouse, M. and Florian, L. (1997) 'Inclusive education in the market place'. *International Journal of Inclusive Education* 1(4): 323–36.

Rowe, K.J. and Hill, P.W. (1994) 'Multilevel modelling in school effectiveness research: how many levels?' Paper presented at the International Congress for School Effectiveness and Improvement, Melbourne, Australia, 3–6 January 1995.

Runnymede Trust (1997) *Islamophobia: Its features and dangers*. London: Runnymede Trust.

Rutter, M., Maughan, B., Mortimore, P. and Ouston, J. (1979) *Fifteen Thousand Hours: Secondary schools and their effects on children*. London: Open Books.

Sailor, W. (1996) 'New structures and systems change for comprehensive positive behavioral support', in L.K. Koegel, R.L. Koegel and G. Dunlap (eds) *Positive Behavioral Support: Including people with difficult behavior in the community*. Baltimore: Paul H. Brookes: 163–206.

Sailor, W., Kleinhammer-Tramill, J., Skrtic, T. and Oas, B.K. (1996) 'Family participation in new community schools', in G.H.S. Singer, L.E. Powers and A.L. Olson (eds) *Redefining Family Support: Innovations in public–private partnerships*. Baltimore: Paul H. Brookes: 313–32.

Salend, S.J. and Duhaney, L.M.G. (1999) 'The impact of inclusion on students with and without disabilities and their educators'. *Remedial and Special Education* 20: 114–26.

Salisbury, J. and Jackson, D. (1996) *Challenging Macho Values*. London: Falmer.

Sammons, P. (1994) 'Findings from school effectiveness research: some implications for improving the quality of schools', in P. Ribbins and E. Burridge (eds) *Improving Education: The issue in quality*. London: Cassell.

—— (1996) 'Complexities in the judgement of school effectiveness'. *Educational Research and Evaluation* 2(2): 113–49.

—— (1999) *School Effectiveness: Coming of age in the 21st century*. Lisse: Swets and Zeitlinger.

Sammons, P., Hillman, J. and Mortimore, P. (1995) *Key Characteristics of Effective Schools: A review of school effectiveness research*. London: Ofsted.

Sammons, P., Hillman, J. and Mortimore, P. (1996) 'Key characteristics of effective schools: a response to "Peddling feel-good fictions"'. *Forum* 38(3): 88–90.

Sammons, P., Nuttall, D. and Cuttance, P. (1993) 'Differential school effectiveness: results from a re-analysis of the Inner London Education Authority's Junior School Project'. *British Educational Research Journal* 19: 381–405.

Sammons, P., Power, S., Whitty, G., Robertson, P., Campbell, C. and Elliot, K. (2000) 'Evaluating the New Community Schools Initiative in Scotland: Briefing Paper 1'. Paper presented to the European Educational Research Association Annual Conference, Edinburgh, 20–3 September.

Sammons, P. and Reynolds, D. (1997) 'A partisan evaluation – John Elliott on school effectiveness'. *Cambridge Journal of Education* 27(1): 123–36.

Sammons, P., Thomas, S. and Mortimore, P. (1997) *Forging Links: Effective schools and effective departments*. London: Paul Chapman.

Sammons, P., Thomas, S., Mortimore, P., Owen, C. and Pennell, H. (1994) *Assessing School Effectiveness: Developing measures to put school performance in context*. London: Ofsted/Institute of Education, University of London.

Saunders, L. (1999) 'A brief history of educational "value added": how did we get to where we are?' *School Effectiveness and School Improvement* 10(2): 233–56.

SCCC (1996) *Teaching for Effective Learning*. Dundee: Scottish Consultative Council on the Curriculum.

Scheerens, J. (1992) *Effective Schooling: Research, theory and practice*. London: Cassell.

Scheerens, J. and Bosker, R. (1997) *The Foundations of Educational Effectiveness*. Oxford: Pergamon.

Scheerens, J., Bosker, R. and Creemers, B.P.M (2001) 'Time for self-criticism: on the viability of school effectiveness research'. *School Effectiveness and School Improvement* 12(1): 131–58.

Scruggs, T.E. and Mastropieri, M.A. (1996) 'Teacher perceptions of mainstreaming/ inclusion, 1958–1995: a research synthesis'. *Exceptional Children* 63: 59–74.

Sebba, J. and Ainscow, M. (1996) 'International developments in inclusive schooling: mapping the issues'. *Cambridge Journal of Education* 26(1): 5–18.

Sebba, J. and Sachdev, D. (1997) *What Works in Inclusive Education?* Ilford: Barnardos.

SEU (1998) *Truancy and School Exclusion Report by the Social Exclusion Unit.* Cm 3957. London: Social Exclusion Unit.

—— (2001) *Preventing Social Exclusion.* London: Social Exclusion Unit.

Sewell, T. (1997) *Black Masculinities and Schooling: How Black boys survive modern schooling.* Stoke-on-Trent: Trentham.

—— (1998) 'Loose canons: exploding the myth of the "black macho" lad', in D. Epstein, J. Elwood, V. Hey and J. Maw (eds) *Failing Boys? Issues in gender and achievement.* Buckingham: Open University Press.

Shaver, D., Golan, S. and Wagner, M. (1996) 'connecting schools and communities through interagency collaboration for school-linked services', in J.G. Cibulka and W.J. Kritek (eds) *Coordination among Schools, Families and Communities.* Albany: State University of New York Press.

Silver, H. (1994) *Good Schools, Effective Schools: Judgements and their histories.* London: Cassell.

Simpson, M. (1999) 'Diagnostic and formative assessment in the Scottish classroom', in T. Bryce and W. Humes (eds) *Scottish Education.* Edinburgh: Edinburgh University Press.

Simpson, M. and Ure, J. (1993) *What's the Difference? A study of differentiation in Scottish secondary schools.* Aberdeen: Northern College.

Siraj-Blatchford, I. (1994) *The Early Years: Laying the foundations for racial equality.* Stoke-on-Trent: Trentham.

Skelton, C. (ed.) (1989) *Whatever Happens to Little Women? Gender and primary schooling.* Milton Keynes: Open University Press.

Skidmore, D. (1999) 'Relationships between contracting discourses of learning difficulty'. *European Journal of Special Needs Education* 14(1): 12–20.

Slavin, R.E. (1996) *Education for All.* Lisse: Swets and Zeitlinger.

Slee, R. (1997) 'Editorial: supporting an international interdisciplinary research conversation'. *International Journal of Inclusive Education* 1(1): i–iv.

—— (1998) 'The politics of theorising special education', in C. Clark, A. Dyson and A. Millward (eds) *Theorising Special Education.* London: Routledge.

Slee, R. and Weiner, G. (2001) 'Education reform and reconstruction as a challenge to research genres: reconsidering school effectiveness research and inclusive schooling', *School Effectiveness and School Improvement* 12(1): 83–98.

Smith, D. and Tomlinson, S. (1989) *The School Effect: A study of multi-racial comprehensives.* London: Policy Studies Institute.

Smithmier, A.M. (1997) 'Aggregative or integrative school-linked services?

Attempting to link an integrative reform design with an aggregative school organizational design'. Paper presented to the Annual Meeting of the American Educational Research Association, Chicago, IL, 24–8 March.

Smyth, E. (1999) *Do Schools Differ? Academic and personal development among pupils in the second-level sector*. Dublin: Economic and Social Research Council.

Solomos, J. and Back, L. (1996) *Racism and Society*. London: Macmillan.

Sostris (1997) *Social Exclusion in Comparative Perspective: Social strategies in risk societies* (Sostris Working Paper 1). London: University of East London, Centre for Biography in Social Policy.

Spender, D. (1984) *Invisible Women: The schooling scandal*. London: Writers and Readers.

Stainback, W. and Stainback, S. (1989) 'Practical organisational strategies', in S. Stainback, W. Stainback and M. Forest (eds) *Educating All Students in the Mainstream of Education*. Baltimore: Brookes.

Standing, K. (1999) 'Lone mothers and "parental involvement": a contradiction in policy?' *Journal of Social Policy* 28(3): 479–96.

Stanley, J. (1993) 'Sex and the quiet schoolgirl', in P. Woods and M. Hammersley (eds) *Gender and Ethnicity in Schools: Ethnographic accounts*. London: Routledge.

Stanley, L. and Wise, S. (1993) *Breaking Out Again: Feminist ontology and epistemology*. London: Routledge.

Stanworth, M. (1988) *Gender and Schooling: A study of sexual divisions in the classroom*. London: Hutchinson/Explorations in Feminism Collective.

Stobart, G., Elwood, J., Hayden, M., White, J. and Mason, K. (1992) *Differential Performance in Examinations at 16+: English and mathematics*. London: University of London Examinations and Assessment Council.

Stoll, L. and Fink, D. (1994) 'Views from the field: linking school effectiveness and school improvement'. *School Effectiveness and School Improvement* 5(2): 149–77.

Stoll, L. and Fink, D. (1996) *Changing Our Schools: Linking school effectiveness and school improvement*. Buckingham: Open University Press.

Stoll, L. and Myers, K. (eds) (1997) *No Quick Fixes*. London: Falmer.

Stringfield, S. (1994) 'A model of elementary school effects', in D. Reynolds *et al.* (eds) *Advances in School Effectiveness Research and Practice*. Oxford: Pergamon.

Stringfield, S., Ross, S. and Smith, L. (1996) *Bold Plans for School Restructuring: The new American schools design*. Mahwah, NJ: Lawrence Erlbaum.

Stringfield, S., Winfield, L., Millsap, M., Puma, M., Gamse, B. and Randall, B. (1994) *Special Strategies for Educating Disadvantaged Children: First year report*. Washington: US Department of Education.

Sukhnandan, L. (1999) *An Investigation into Gender Differences in Achievement – Phase 1: A review of recent research and LEA information on provision*. Slough: NFER.

Sukhnandan, L., Lee, B. and Kelleher, S. (2000) *An Investigation into Gender Differences in Achievement -Phase 2: School and classroom strategies.* Slough: NFER.

Swann, Lord (1985) *Education for All: Final Report of the Committee of Inquiry into the Education of Children from Ethnic Minority Groups.* Cmnd 9453. London: HMSO.

Sylva, K., Sammons, P., Melhuish, E., Siraj-Blatchford, I. and Taggart, B. (1999) *An Introduction to the EPPE Project* (Effective Provision of Pre-School Education Project Technical Paper 1). London: Institute of Education, University of London.

Taggart, B. and Sammons, P. (1999) 'Evaluating the impact of a raising school standards initiative', in R. Bosker, B. Creemers and S. Stringfield (eds) *Enhancing Educational Excellence, Equity and Efficiency: Evidence from evaluations of systems and schools in change.* Dordrecht: Kluwer.

Taylor, M.J. with Hegarty, S. (1985) *The Best of Both Worlds? A review of research into the education of pupils of South Asian origin.* Windsor: NFER-Nelson.

Teddlie, C. (1994a) 'The study of context in school effects research: history, methods, results and theoretical implications', in D. Reynolds *et al.* (eds) *Advances in School Effectiveness Research and Practice.* Oxford: Pergamon.

—— (1994b) 'The integration of classroom and school process data in school effectiveness research', in D. Reynolds *et al.* (eds) *Advances in School Effectiveness Research and Practice.* Oxford: Pergamon.

Teddlie, C. and Reynolds, D. (2000) *The International Handbook of School Effectiveness Research.* London: Falmer.

Teddlie, C. and Reynolds, D. (2001) 'Countering the critics: responses to recent criticisms of school effectiveness research'. *School Effectiveness and School Improvement* 12(1): 41–82.

Thomas, G. (1997) 'Inclusive schools for an inclusive society'. *British Journal of Special Education* 24(3): 103–7.

Thomas, G. and Loxley, A. (2001) *Deconstructing Special Education and Constructing Inclusion.* Buckingham: Open University Press.

Thomas, G., Walker, D. and Webb, J. (1998) *The Making of the Inclusive School.* London: Routledge.

Thomas, S. and Mortimore, P. (1996) 'Comparison of value-added models for secondary-school effectiveness'. *Research Papers in Education* 11(1): 5–33.

Thomas, S., Sammons, P., Mortimore, P. and Smees, R. (1997) 'Stability and consistency in secondary schools' effects on students' GCSE outcomes over 3 Years'. *School Effectiveness and School Improvement* 8: 169–97.

Thrupp, M. (1999) *Schools Making a Difference: Let's be realistic!* Buckingham: Open University Press.

—— (2001) 'Sociological and political concerns about school effectiveness research: time for a new research agenda'. *School Effectiveness and School Improvement* 12(1): 7–40.

Tizard, B., Blatchford, P., Burke, J., Farquhar, C. and Plewis, I. (1988) *Young Children at School in the Inner City*. Hove: Lawrence Erlbaum.

Tomlinson, S. (1983) *Ethnic Minorities in British Schools: A review of the literature, 1960–1982*. London: Routledge and Kegan Paul.

—— (1990) *Multicultural Education in White Schools*. London: Batsford.

Townsend, T. (2001) 'Satan or saviour? An analysis of two decades of school effectiveness research'. *School Effectiveness and School Improvement* 12(1): 115–30.

Townsend, T., Clarke, P. and Ainscow, M. (eds) (1999) *Third Millennium Schools A World of Difference in Effectiveness and Improvement*. Lisse: Swets and Zeitlinger.

Troyna, B. (1993) *Racism and Education: Research perspectives*. Buckingham: Open University Press.

Troyna, B. and Carrington, B. (1990) *Education, Racism and Reform*. London: Routledge.

Troyna, B. and Siraj-Blatchford, I. (1993) 'Providing support or denying access? The experiences of students designated as "ESL" and "SN" in a multi-ethnic secondary school'. *Educational Review* 45(1): 3–11.

Troyna, B. and Vincent, C. (1995) 'The discourses of social justice'. *Discourse: Studies in the Cultural Politics of Education* 16(2): 149–66.

UNESCO (1988) *Review of the Present Situation in Special Needs Education*. Paris: UNESCO.

—— (1994) *The Salamanca Statement and Framework for Action on Special Needs Education*. Paris: UNESCO.

—— (1995) *Review of the Present Situation in Special Needs Education*. Paris: UNESCO.

United States Department of Education (1986) *What Works: Research about teaching and learning*. Washington: United States Department of Education.

Vaughn, S. and Schumm, J. (1995) 'Responsible inclusion for students with learning disabilities'. *Journal of Learning Disabilities* 28: 264–70.

Vaughn, S., Schumm, J., Jallard, B. and Slusher, J. (1996) 'Teachers' views of inclusion'. *Learning Disabilities: Research and Practice* 11: 96–106.

Vialli, L., Cooper, D. and Franks, L. (1997) 'Professional development schools and equity: a critical analysis of rhetoric and research', in W.M. Apple (ed.) *Review of Research in Education*, Vol. 22. Washington: American Educational Research Association.

Vincent, C. (1996) *Parents and Teachers: Power and participation*. London: Falmer.

—— (2000) *Including Parents?: Citizenship, education and parental agency.* Buckingham: Open University Press.

Vincent, C. and Martin, J. (2000) 'School-based parents' groups: a politics of voice and representation.' *Journal of Education Policy* 15(5): 459–80.

Vincent, C., Martin, J. and Ranson, S. (1999) "'Little polities": schooling, governance and parental participation'. End of award report to the ESRC.

Vincent, C. and Tomlinson, S. (1997) 'Home–school relationships: "the swarming of disciplinary mechanisms"?' *British Educational Research Journal* 23(3): 361–77.

Vincent, C. and Warren, S. (1998) 'Becoming a "better" parent? Motherhood, education and transition'. *British Journal of Sociology of Education* 19(2): 177–93.

Wade, B. and Moore, M. (2000) 'Starting early with books', in S. Wolfendale and J. Bastiani (eds) *The Contributions of Parents to School Effectiveness.* London: David Fulton.

Walkerdine, V. (1988) *The Mastery of Reason.* London: Routledge.

Walkerdine, V. and the Girls and Mathematics Unit (1989) *Counting Girls Out.* London: Virago.

Wang, M.C. and Baker, E.T. (1985–6) 'Mainstreaming programs: design features and effects'. *Journal of Special Education* 19: 503–21.

Wang, M.C., Haertel, G.D. and Walberg, H.J. (1998a) *Effective Features of Collaborative, School-linked Services for Children in Elementary Schools: What do we know from research and practice?* (Publication Series no.2). Mid-Atlantic Laboratory for Student Success, Temple University, USA, www.temple.edu/LSS/pub98-2.htm.

Wang, M.C., Haertel, G.D. and Walberg, H.J. (1998b) *The Effectiveness of Collaborative School-linked Services* (Publication Series no.1). Mid-Atlantic Laboratory for Student Success, Temple University, USA, www.temple.edu/LSS/pub98-1.htm.

Warren, C. (1999) 'Lessons from the evaluation of New Jersey's School-based Youth Services Program'. Paper presented at the Improving Results for Children and Families by Connecting Collaborative Services with School Reform Efforts, Washington, 26–7 January.

Warren, S. (1997) 'Who do these boys think they are? An investigation into the construction of masculinities in a primary classroom'. *International Journal of Inclusive Education* 1(2): 207–22.

Watkins, C., Whitty, G., Rivers, K. and Kemp, S. (2000) *The Healthier School Partnership 1996–99: Report of the Evaluation Support Team.* London: Institute of Education, University of London.

Wedell, K. (1993) 'Special Needs Education: The next 25 years', in *National Commission on Education Briefings.* London: Heinemann.

Weekes, D. and Wright, C. (1999) *Improving Practice: A whole school approach to raising the achievement of African Caribbean youth.* London: Runnymede Trust in association with Nottingham Trent University.

Weiner, G. (1990) 'Developing educational policy on gender in the primary school: the contribution of teachers in the United Kingdom', in G. Weiner (ed.) *The Primary School and Equal Opportunities – International perspectives on gender issues.* London: Cassell.

—— (1994) *Feminism in Education: An introduction.* Buckingham: Open University Press.

Wendel, T. (2000) *Creating Equity and Quality: A literature review of school effectiveness and improvement* (Society for the Advancement of Excellence in Education Research Series 6). Kelowna, BC: Society for the Advancement of Excellence in Education.

West, M. and Hopkins, D. (1996) 'Reconceptualising school effectiveness and school improvement'. Paper presented at the School Effectiveness and Improvement Symposium of the Annual Conference of the American Educational Research Association, New York, 8 April.

Wexler, P. (1992) *Becoming Somebody: Towards a social psychology of school.* London: Falmer.

White, J. and Barber, M. (eds) (1997) *Perspectives on School Effectiveness Improvement* (Bedford Way Papers). London: Institute of Education, University of London.

Whitty, G. (1985) *Sociology and School Knowledge: Curriculum theory, research and politics.* London: Methuen.

—— (1997) 'Creating quasi-markets in education: a review of recent research on parental choice and school autonomy in three countries', in M. Apple (ed.) *Review of Research in Education*, 22. Washington: American Educational Research Association.

Whitty, G., Aggleton, P.J., Gamarnikow, E. and Tyrer, P. (1998a) *Education and Health Inequalities.* Input Paper 10 to the Independent Inquiry into Inequalities in Health (chaired by Sir Donald Acheson), January.

Whitty, G., Power, S. and Halpin, D. (1998b) *Devolution and Choice.* London: Routledge.

WHO (1999) *Child-Friendly Schools Checklist.* Geneva: World Health Organisation.

Whyte, J., Deem, R., Kant, L. and Cruckshank, M. (eds) (1985) *Girl Friendly Schooling.* London: Routledge.

Wilcox, B. and Gray, J. (1996) *Inspecting Schools – Holding schools to account and helping schools to improve.* Buckingham: Open University Press.

Willms, J.D. and Cuttance, P. (1985) 'School effects in Scottish secondary schools'. *British Journal of Sociology of Education* 6(3): 289–305.

Wilson, J. (1999) 'Some conceptual difficulties about "inclusion"'. *Support for Learning* 14(3): 110–12.

—— (2000) 'Doing justice to inclusion'. *European Journal of Special Needs Education* 15(3): 297–304.

Witziers, B. (1994) 'Coordination in secondary schools and its implications for student achievement'. Paper presented at the annual conference of the American Educational Research Association, New Orleans, 4–8 April.

Wolfendale, S. and Bastiani, J. (eds) (2000) *The Contribution of Parents to School Effectiveness*. London: David Fulton.

Wolfendale, S. and Crisp, A. (1996) 'Evaluation of Tower Hamlets SEN Parent Partnership Scheme'. Report to the London Borough of Tower Hamlets.

Wolfensberger, W. (1972) *Normalisation*. Toronto: National Institute on Mental Retardation.

Wright, C. (1986) 'School processes – an ethnographic study', in J. Eggleston, D. Dunn and M. Anjali (1986) *Education for Some: The educational and vocational experiences of 15–18 year old members of minority ethnic groups*. Stoke-on-Trent: Trentham.

—— (1992) *Race Relations in the Primary School*. London: David Fulton.

Wright, C., Weekes, D. and McGlaughlin, A. (2000) *'Race', Class and Gender in Exclusions from School*. London: Falmer.

Yell, M.L. (1998) 'The legal basis of inclusion'. *Educational Leadership* 56: 70–3.

Young, I. (1990) *Justice and the Politics of Difference*. Princetown: Princeton University Press.

Zetlin, A.G. (1998) *Lessons Learned about Integrating Services* (Publication Series no. 98-4). Mid-Atlantic Laboratory for Student Success, Temple University, USA, www.temple.edu/LSS/pub98-4.htm.

**Appendix 1:** *Strategies and features of inclusive schools*

| Strategies | Features |
|---|---|
| *Monitoring and evaluation integral* | Local and national monitoring vital;<br>Rigorous monitoring sensitive to the differential experiences of different groups, e.g. based on analysis of 'race', gender, special educational needs, and socio-economic status;<br>Range of processes and outcomes monitored, e.g. attendance, exclusion, subject choice, attainment, staying on rates and leaver destinations;<br>Need for systematic national and local evaluations;<br>Development of appropriate 'inclusive school' self-evaluation. |
| *Inclusive leadership* | Commitment to 'inclusive schooling';<br>Developing shared 'inclusive leadership' throughout school;<br>Inclusive vision;<br>Promotes equity;<br>Opposes discrimination and disadvantage;<br>Promotes inclusive principles, policies and practices;<br>Acts as role model. |
| *Inclusive whole school ethos and culture* | Promoting 'inclusive schooling';<br>Focus on equity;<br>Shared vision and goals. |
| *High expectations for all pupils* | Underachievement is unacceptable for any group of pupils;<br>Awareness and development of teacher expectations and attitudes;<br>Awareness and development of pupil expectations and attitudes;<br>Emphasis on pupil achievements not 'problems'. |
| *Valuing pupil perspectives and involvement* | Integral to development of inclusive policies and practices;<br>Importance of pupil voice in school processes and decision-making. |

*Appendix 1 Continued*

| *Clear and consistent whole school policies* | Inclusive policies; Addressing disadvantage and discrimination; Promoting equity; Emphasis on early intervention and prevention; Consistent on issues of harassment, behaviour and attendance; Integral to School Development Plan. |
|---|---|
| *Promotion of inclusive learning and teaching strategies* | Child-centred learning and teaching; Inclusive formal and informal curricula; Inclusive non-discriminatory curricula and assessment across all subject areas; Attention to curriculum coverage; Inclusive pedagogy and teaching methods; Encourages parental involvement and support. |
| *Inclusive classroom structures and practices* | Attention to whole class teaching and within class groupings; Structured and interactive whole class teaching; Mixed ability grouping; Appropriate individual differentiation. |
| *Additional supports for pupils and staff* | Provided as necessary and appropriate; Relating to academic and pastoral supports for pupils; Support for staff developing and implementing inclusive learning and teaching strategies. |
| *Recognition and respect for community languages* | Development of English as an Additional Language approaches; Importance of community languages in communications with parents/ carers. |
| *Inclusive staff collaboration and teamwork* | Relating to classrooms and inter-agency collaboration; Need for clear role relationships among different professionals working together; Development of inclusive collaboration processes. |

*Appendix 1 Continued*

| | |
|---|---|
| *Positive action to promote good social relationships* | Throughout the school, involving interactions with pupils and staff; Development of pupils' inter-personal skills; Personal, social and health education; Sex and relationships education; Positive pupil behaviour ; Recognition of peer group influence. |
| *Inclusive communication* | Open and accessible throughout school, including staff and pupils, with parents and other agencies as appropriate. |
| *Inclusive parental involvement* | Developing appropriate and inclusive home–school links; Engaging parents and families in schools and education; Development of two-way communication; Recognition of community languages; Support from parents/carers for schools; Support to parents/carers from schools. |
| *Inclusive inter-school collaboration* | Developing collaboration between schools to promote inclusive policies and practices; e.g. primary/ secondary links and transfers; Cluster arrangements for SEN. |
| *Inclusive inter-agency collaboration* | Holistic approach to pupil development and children's services; Attention to pupil's physical, emotional, mental, social and educational development; Healthy schools; Tackling barriers to learning and developing processes to enable learning for pupils and parents/carers. |
| *Inclusive community involvement* | Strengthening linkages between school and local communities; Support from the community for the school; Support from the school to the community; School as a community resource. |

*Appendix 1 Continued*

| *Provision of adequate financial and other resources* | Funding and personnel to develop inclusive schooling; Issues of sustainability acknowledged. |
| --- | --- |
| *Continuing professional development* | Range of training opportunities for all staff involved; Considering principles, practices, processes and outcomes associated with inclusive schooling; Multi-disciplinary and inter-agency joint training where appropriate; In longer term, relevant development of initial teacher education (and other appropriate professionals' training) to incorporate inclusive schooling. |